Sales Effort and Marketing Strategy:
A Systems Approach

Sales Effort
and Marketing Strategy:
A Systems Approach

Richard V. Butt

American Management Association, Inc.

Standard book number: 8144-2128-8
Library of Congress catalog card number: 76-93789

To Pamela

and in memory
of my father

Foreword

Aᴍᴇʀɪᴄᴀ is the home of great marketing men. The art of selling is practiced by the average American as a natural occupation. The life story of the professional salesman has shaped the nation and given the country a marketing character of which people in other parts of the world have been both critical and approving, but which they have definitely recognized. American marketers have been successful, and in the world of commerce it is results that count. There is less controversy over whether American marketers are the greatest than over why they are great—a far more complex question. Marketing is basically a war game whose process includes analysis, synthesis, and action. The successful marketer who plays the game is shrewd, assertive, clever, and wise; is able to recognize opportunities, formulate plans, and act with power. Because marketing is a game of war, its theoreticians have rarely held the stage. Most books that are read by and have an impact on marketing men are written by successful marketers, who assume that the proof of theory is action and that the ineffective theory or the theory not acted upon is not worth talking about. But the successful marketer generally turns to writing long after his prime, when his books tend to be memoirs that are out of date.

It is intended that this book be neither a memoir nor a theoretical exercise. My objective has been to evaluate the current state of the art and to set forth a series of plans to advance it. I am interested in change because there is much to be improved in the current system. Most of all, I am against bad sales effort management because it is a waste of human resources. The marketing system faces a serious challenge in the rising tide of individualism and the expanding economic opportunities in the free world, a situation reflected in the rising salesman turnover rate in most companies. Salesmen will not suffer under bad management; they will leave to find a well-managed marketing organization. It is hoped that this book will focus attention on the subject of sales effort management and the use of marketing strategy; and that marketing men, like any well-designed adaptive systems, will change to meet the challenge of the future.

RICHARD V. BUTT

Contents

1

The Systems Approach
to Marketing Staffing

THE marketing staffing problem relates to the field salesman, to head office marketing strategists, and to the management in control of these two groups. It can be defined in terms of:

1. Recruiting, hiring, and training salesmen.
2. Determining how many salesmen should be hired and where they should be located.
3. Selecting salesmen's territories in terms of number of accounts, profit potential, call frequency, and other logistics.
4. Deciding how much time each salesman should spend on soliciting customers, traveling, writing reports, and managing territories.

5. Determining how the salesman's effort should be applied by product.
6. Calculating the quantitative relationship of sales effort and other competitive weapons to sales performance and marketing strategy.
7. Analyzing the performance of the salesman and the marketing system in order to change and improve the system.

The marketing strategist is concerned with choosing a set of competitive weapons and using them in various weights to effect a desired marketing system performance. These weapons include price, advertising, technical support, distribution capability, and sales effort (in terms of time and effectiveness). Although the main focus of this book will be on sales effort, this particular weapon must be related to the marketing strategist's total weapon mix.

The basic marketing staffing problem has been faced by thousands of marketing managers since the beginning of commercial business. Many books and articles have been written to offer assistance, but the published literature on the subject, for the most part, has not been very innovative. One would expect that over the course of time the problem would have been attacked and solved in numerous ways; that an approach like "send out some salesmen and see what happens" would be regarded as a humorous relic of ancient sales managers who had long ago signed their last expense account. Unfortunately, those tactics are still very much alive and are used, not only by small, out-of-date firms, but by the largest and most powerful corporations. There have been flourishes of interest in the subject (the middle 1950s was probably the last), but in general, marketing literature has not advanced the field appreciably.

This book, which was evolved over a six-year period (1963–69) during the author's employment with one of the world's largest companies, reflects, in essence, the application of modern management technology to the marketing staffing problem. Management technology refers to the development and implementation of the systems approach, advanced strategic planning, operations research, and computer technology. In evolving his study, the author was fortunate to be associated with many experts in modern management technology, to have access to the latest computer equipment, and to have time to experiment with a successful line marketing activity.

This book includes both a generalized case study and a series of expositions on the theoretical underpinnings of marketing activity. The author recognizes that the problem is complex, but believes that the new approach can lead to substantial improvements in marketing organization performance. Certainly, the cost of ignoring new approaches in the marketing field can be very high.

The marketing staffing problem can be explained in the form of a series of questions to the marketing manager; if he can answer all these questions without hestitation, he probably has a very well-thought-out staffing system. The purpose of this book is to be of assistance in developing such a system.

The Marketing Staffing Test

A. Hiring and Training

1. How do you recruit and hire salesmen? Are they expected to be salesmen only, or salesmen in preparation for management?

2. Are the salesman candidates chosen with regard to a specific sales territory or product line?

3. How do your hired sales candidates compare with those of your chief competitors? Do your competitors hire experienced veterans or recent college graduates?

4. How do you train sales candidates? How much is spent on their training?

5. What is the trade-off between previous salesman experience and required training?

6. How much do your competitors spend on training?

B. Deployment

1. How many salesmen do you have totally? by geographic area?

2. How is this number related to your sales performance goals? If you had more salesmen, could you sell more, or would the extra salesmen not be able to pull their own weight?

3. How do you decide where to locate salesmen?

4. Are all your salesmen about equal in terms of numbers of accounts? product sales potential? profit potential?

C. Sales Effort

1. How much time does each salesman spend in calling on customers, traveling, and managing his territory?

2. How do you determine the optimal salesman call frequency? If he called one more or one less time per month, what would the effect be on sales?

3. How do salesmen divide up their sales time by product? Is the sales time devoted to each prod-

uct related to sales goals? to profit contribution?

4. If your sales force increased its calls by 10 percent on your ten key products, what would be the percent increase in sales volume? in profit?

5. How does your competitor manage sales effort? Do you monitor competitor changes in sales efforts? How?

6. According to your knowledge of the sales effectiveness of your staff and that of your competitor, if you increased sales effort by 10 percent and your competitor increased sales effort by 12 percent, who would win?

D. Other Weapons

1. Assume that you used sales effort to gain a new account, and your competitor reduced price. Who would get the account if you did not meet the price? if you did?

2. Assume that you used sales effort. Who would win if your competitor stepped up advertising? offered technical assistance? improved distribution capability?

3. If you are competing with five companies, you increase sales effort by 10 percent, Competitor A increases advertising expenditures by 5 percent, Competitor B reduces price by 2 percent, Competitor C spends $10,000 for a better delivery system, Competitor D volunteers to spend $8,000 on a technical assistance project, and Competitor E increases sales effort by 8 percent—who would win?

If the last question appears to involve a dreadfully complex decision, it should be recognized that as marketing manager you and your staff make that decision many times each day, although in most instances the decision is not so clearly outlined. For example, a district manager's telling his salesman, "Go take that buyer to lunch next week and press for an order" represents an extra call and a certain percent increase in sales effort. The good district manager is thinking in terms of the salesman, the buyer, the competitor, and the competitor's choice of weapon; perhaps he is aware of his competitor's superior delivery capability or more effective salesman. By changing sales effort, he is attempting to trip the balance in his own company's favor. The poor district manager, on the other hand, may not be alert to many of these factors; the extra call may be his cure-all for any situation when the orders are not coming in. Sometimes he will win and at other times he will lose, but he will certainly lose more often than the alert manager. And his losses are the company's losses.

Modern management technology should be applied to solve the marketing staffing problem. Four specific aspects of this modern management technology are:

- The systems approach.
- Advanced strategic planning.
- Operations research.
- Computer technology.

Let us examine these four subjects and relate them to the marketing problem.

The Systems Approach

It has been noted by various authorities that the systems approach should be regarded as a frame of mind, as a useful way of thinking, and as applied common sense. These terse descriptions, while doing little to explain the method, point out a unique aspect of the systems approach—its universality. It has been applied to such divergent projects as the development of complex military war devices and the welfare programs of large urban communities, although, to a significant extent, it has been most widely used in aerospace and military applications. Because a large proportion of this activity is carried out under security, the literature on the subject has reached the outer world in an osmotic fashion. The more progressive corporations, particularly those involved in defense activities, have been aware of the developments within the applied systems area; however, it does not appear that the approach has been utilized to any significant extent by industry to date. In general, the modern corporation has created a large number of departments entitled "Business Systems" or "Systems Analysis" and has populated these departments with men whom it calls "Systems Analysts." Neither the departments nor the individual titles obscure the fact that systems work is not being done, except in the most trivial sense.

The systems approach was developed to help in the systematic analysis of complex problems, generally concerned with the uncertainty of predicting future environment, and with the probabilistic rather than deterministic structure of a given system. If the systems within which businessmen must operate are necessarily complex, then the systems approach can be of great potential benefit to the modern corporation. Therefore, we have chosen this approach to attack the problem of the employment of field sales manpower in a marketing environment. But first let us examine the language of the method so that practitioners will encounter a minimum of translation difficulties.

System. Various analysts have concluded that a system is (1) an organized or complex whole, (2) any collection of entities that can be understood as forming a coherent group, and (3) an organized collection of interrelated elements characterized by a boundary and functional unity.

Unity, organization, coherence, and interrelationship have been stressed in this definition of the system. However, it is important to recognize that there are relatively disorganized systems as well. Therefore, the marketing manager in an industrial concern should not only be in search of the good systems that are organized, unified, coherent, and interrelated, but should be aware that the main purpose of systems design is to develop or increase the desirable attributes of existing corporate systems. It is important to recognize that systems are not built out of thin air; the existence of a system, however poorly understood, is the raw material of systems design.

If we accept these general definitions of the system, we can agree that the U.S. government and IBM are systems, that a boy hitting a baseball is a system (extremely complex, it turns out), and that the process by which the number of salesmen in a field sales organization is chosen is also a system. By this approach we can begin to appraise the ultimate strength of the systems method, which seeks a common ground between systems that vary widely in their objectives but are similar in that they both do have objectives.

Boundary. The concept of boundary is a natural way of separating out systems from a larger system. The universe could be considered a gigantic system, yet if it were considered the only system, our ability to understand even that single system would be very limited. The division of systems allows the analyst to concentrate on a more manageable problem because it is within a reasonable realm of control. The boundary is often referred to as the "interface," since it represents an area of contact between one system and another.

Environment. Environment can be considered the area surrounding the system and is often referred to as the "embedding" environment. The system is never isolated; it must always interact with the embedding environment. An important aspect of the systems approach is the prediction of future environment in which the proposed system will be embedded.

The Goodwin model. In his course on management systems, Dr. W. R. Goodwin of the New York University Graduate School of Business develops an operating system description that focuses on some of the more difficult areas of system design encountered in practical applications (see Exhibit 1). The method begins with a clear statement of the desired system missions, goals, and objectives. It is important at this stage to define our missions in meaningful terms rather than in trite or ambiguous phrases such as "maximize profits"; if we are to design a system to carry out a mission, we must be able to relate specific operating procedures to a specific mission.

The Goodwin model includes an analysis of the current system. In such an analysis, some of the questions to be asked are: "What is the current system's mission?" "How does it seek to achieve that mission?" "Is it successful, and if not, why not?" "When does the system act?" "Where does the system operate?" "Why are we operating with the current system?" The system must also be analyzed with regard to the constraints on it. If it is a manpower staffing system, there might be a constraint on the funds available for salaries or on the number of people allowed to be employed in a given area.

Exhibit 1
The Goodwin Model

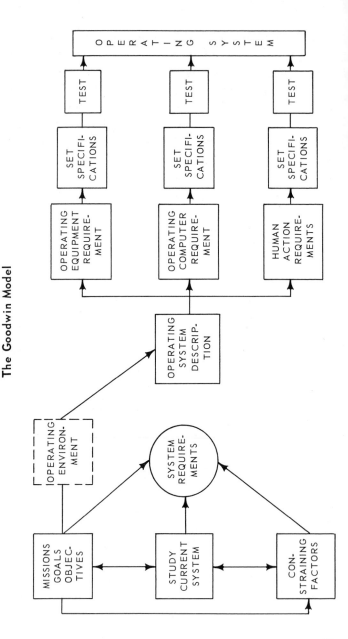

The stages of mission setting, current system analysis, and analysis of constraints culminate in the statement of system requirements. The analyst asks, "What do you want the system to do?" The reply might be, "To forecast annually the optimal number of salesmen in the next three-year period." It might also be, "To deliver X tons of nuclear ordnance on a target of Y square miles from an altitude of Z thousand feet."

It is essential that the design of the future system consider future environment and future constraints. A common failing in practice is to assume that the current environment will be the future environment. In military systems design, the time span between design and operation is so long that if the designer is not accurate in predicting the future environment, the weapon system may be obsolete even as it rolls off the assembly line. Similar time spans are involved in the problems of researching, developing, producing, and marketing a new product in industries subject to a high degree of technological obsolescence, such as chemicals or electronics; yet the typical business planners in these industries do not often recognize the parallel.

Finally, the system design is embodied in an operating system description. The questions of why, what, how, where, and when are answered at this stage. The operating system is divided according to required resources: (1) operating equipment requirements, (2) operating computer requirements, and (3) human action requirements. The most difficult part of the system design is to divide the operations so that resources are allocated in an efficient manner. One criterion that can be used is cost-benefit; that is, choosing the lowest-cost-greatest-benefit function. For example, if we were concerned with the repetitive addition of a series of data it would probably be less costly to use a computer. Here we deal with "minimum cost for equal benefits."

Once the system operations have been divided into resource sectors, a detailed set of specifications is written for each element; the elements are then tested individually and as a total system; and finally, the operating system is constructed.

The cybernetic model. Before exploring the cybernetic model, we must explain what cybernetics is and why it is applicable in the context of systems design. Cybernetics is a science. Norbert Weiner of M.I.T. is the founder of this science and describes it as "the science of communication and control in the animal and the machine."[1] It is important to recognize that the study of communication and control is related to systems design; that, in fact, communication and control are the two main aspects of the system in its operational context.

It may appear unusual that animate and inanimate organizations are given similar treatment, until we recall that our definition of system could be related to both. For example, "the boy hitting a baseball" system involves, not only the physical laws of aerodynamics, but the human feedback and muscular response mechanisms as well. The modern corporation includes, in massive proportions, man-machine systems of extreme complexity. In particular, one of the foundations of the cybernetic approach is the analysis and construction of "ultrastable" systems. Although the word "ultrastable" has the connotation of rigidity, the ultrastable system is anything but rigid.

> An open system, whether social or biological, in a changing environment either changes or perishes. . . . [T]he only avenue to survival is change. The capacity

[1] N. Weiner, *Cybernetics* (New York: Wiley, 1948), p. 1.

to persist through a change of structure and behavior has been called "ultrastability." If a complex social organization is to survive critical changes in this environment, it can do so only by changing its structure and behavior. . . . [A]ny industrial corporation, such as International Business Machines or General Electric, that has survived the last fifty years of social change in the United States has done so through the continuation of original organizational and operational patterns. . . . The concept of ultrastability will aid in distinguishing between systems that achieve stability under specific constant conditions and those that can learn or evolve new structures and behavior so as to remain stable under changing conditions.[2]

The following comments should be made in reference to this statement:

1. Cybernetics deals with "open" systems, that is, systems that have interaction with their *environment*.
2. The ultrastable system has built-in methods of changing its *structure* and *behavior;* it is *self-transforming*.
3. In order to change, the system *learns* about its changing environment.
4. The process of learning and changing is *innovation*.
5. While the ultrastable system is maintaining its existence in the face of a changing environment, it exhibits *purposeful* problem-solving behavior.

[2] M. L. Cadwallader, "The Cybernetic Analysis of Change in Complex Social Organization," in *Communication and Culture,* ed. A. G. Smith (New York: Holt, Rinehart and Winston, Inc., 1966), p. 397.

The parallels between the cybernetic approach and the Goodwin model should be obvious. The Goodwin model emphasizes the importance of predicting future environment and designing operational systems to function in that future environment. The science of cybernetics focuses on making this process continuous.

To the industrial or government planner, the sales manager, and the welfare worker, it is not a revelation that their environments are complex and difficult to pinpoint. However, it may be surprising to them that a science has been developed that applies to such complex environments and does not attempt to solve this particular problem in a deterministic manner. In fact, the forceful adoption of methods that depend on deterministic solutions tend to defeat their original purpose by creating a system that cannot be stable. Just as the Heisenberg Uncertainty Principle shattered the security of scientists who depended on determinism, the new science of cybernetics reveals the uncertainty of complex social and industrial environments. It is important to recognize that cybernetics not only reveals an uncertain world but also suggests a method of dealing with this kind of environment.

The areas covered in designing and building a cybernetic model of a system include the

- Information in the system.
- Communication network.
- Subsystems.
- Feedback mechanisms.
- System operating rules.

The investigator thus directs his attention to communication and control with regard to system structure and behavior.

The cybernetic system is an innovative one, because it includes sensors to the environment, self-adaptive structure, and rules governing behavior to deal with the changing environment. If the rules organizing the problem-solving aspect of the system are well designed, the rate at which the system innovates is increased. Thus the company that quickly analyzes the market's potential product needs, and develops products to meet those needs, will tend to be highly innovative. On the other hand, the company that directs its market research effort to the buggy whip industry will be blind to innovative potentials in the aerospace industry. There is a natural tendency for a company to do tomorrow what it did today; mechanisms must be built into the system that will counteract this tendency and focus on the future, however uncertain the future may be. The higher the technology of the industry, the shorter the time span between product invention and product obsolescence; and hence the more rapid the system's product invention and development processes must be if the system is to survive.

The flow model. The flow model is concerned with the analysis of resource and information flow through a social organization, with particular regard to the decision-making process in the organization. Professor Jay W. Forrester of the M.I.T. School of Industrial Management has developed one such flow model which he includes in his philosophy of "industrial dynamics." In this model, the control aspects are regarded as the essential factors in analyzing and managing the organization. The components of the system include flow paths, resource flows, and control valves.

Industrial dynamics is essentially an introspective process whose emphasis is on the analysis of the current system in terms of flows (not unlike the analysis of an oil refinery in product-engineering terms), with the decision-making function of the organization considered as a control activity. This method is concerned with laying bare the inner workings of the organization and is less concerned with the interaction of that system with the outer environment.

Industrial dynamics is also directed to resolving the potential discrepancies between real and apparent organizational achievements and objectives. A control function is established in parallel with the action-oriented functions to maintain standards of performance and compare the output of the "activating groups" with these standards through a system of monitoring. It should be noted that there is no mention of the outer environment nor is there concern expressed that the standards of performance may not be related to the operating environment. It is assumed that the "real" objectives or standards of performance are not time-dependent and possess a "truth" in themselves. The flow model, then, appears to be the method of describing closed systems.

In search of a unified model. The Goodwin model, the cybernetic model, and the flow model focus upon different aspects of system design. Although the derivation of an "essence" for each of these approaches may be unfair to the designers, it can lead to the design of a better model by clarifying various simplified concepts.

The Goodwin model can provide a general framework for systems design, in which the stages in the design process are clearly drawn. The cybernetic model focuses attention on the time and space dependency of design; the Goodwin model points out what the cybernetic model is directed to as a scientific inquiry; and the flow model provides a way of analyzing the internal system. Therefore,

26

taken as a general model, the three individual models contribute in a unique way to the design of a system.

Advanced Strategic Planning

In the marketing staffing test at the beginning of this chapter, many of the questions referred to the use of competitive weapons: the choice of weapons, the "quantity" of the weapons, and the timing in using the weapons. The concept referred to here is advanced strategic planning, the technology of the marketing strategist. Advanced strategic planning evolved out of U.S. Department of Defense work, which emphasized the use of a formal strategic planning flow chart of events. In marketing, the flow chart proceeds from an information-gathering analysis phase to a goal setting and alternative strategy formulation phase and finally to a strategy implementation and action phase.

Information gathering and analysis. If we expect to survive in the competitive world of marketing, we must have a great deal of information on our own company and on the competition. Since it is generally easier to obtain information on our own company, our first step might be to assemble a data bank relating to our marketing staffing system. A complete list of desirable data is presented in Chapter 2. This same type of information should then be gathered for all major competitors. Since the data bank will probably be incomplete at first, and require an outlay of funds to round it out, the value of the desired information should be carefully weighed against its cost. The data can then be analyzed in order to sift out the important facts and to present the data in a form that is easy to comprehend. If the analysis is competent, many factors relative to the company and its competitors will become evident, including the selective strengths and weaknesses of the company and of each competitor. The basis for formulating a marketing strategy is often to work within the company's strengths to exploit the competitors' weaknesses.

Goal setting and alternative strategies. The next phase often begins with an interrogation of management to determine the goals of the marketing organization. The interrogator, who must develop alternative strategies to accomplish those goals, will quickly recognize that goals like "maximizing profit" are easy to say but impossible to achieve. The goals must be set in concrete terms like "increase sales of product A by 10 percent," or "increase market share by 5 percent." Goal setting is often a frustrating and time-consuming exercise. Nevertheless, it is less taxing than is developing a successful strategy for an unwanted goal.

With a set of concrete goals in mind, the strategist develops a set of alternative strategies. Using the information from phase one, the strategist must follow a rigorous approach in exploiting the competitor's weaknesses. It is not a coincidence that the concept of strategic planning was developed by individuals concerned with military encounters. The technique is used in war games extensively. The marketing strategist is in many ways similar to the general in command of a military force. Although there may be no fatalities of a badly chosen and unsuccessful marketing strategy, there may be many serious casualties.

Finally, after generating a series of alternative strategies to accomplish its goals, management chooses one strategy for implementation.

Strategy implementation and action. Once the strategy and goal have been determined, the strategy must be implemented. It is surprising how often companies fail in this stage. The gathering of data and the round-table discussions on goal setting and strategies may become merely academic, or appear to be aspects of long-range rather than short-range planning. Too often the strategies are not implemented or are implemented after too long a time lapse. But it is essential to take action on schedule, and especially to use the strategy that has been developed. All individuals concerned with the marketing plans must be advised of the new strategy, and constant checks must be made to ensure that the strategy is being carried out.

The perfect execution of this three-phase strategic plan is a great satisfaction to the marketing manager and a bane to the competitor. Before dismissing the use of advanced strategic planning as being too complicated, the wise manager had better know that his competitor feels the same way.

Operations Research

Most modern marketing men have a general awareness of the field of operations research and its work in certain functional areas. However, although the marketing function has been relatively unaffected to date by operations research, in the middle and late 1960s there have been many developments in operations research that are applicable to marketing and should be considered within its framework. Some of the areas in operations research covered in this book include game theory, regression analysis, linear and dynamic programming techniques, and simulation models. They will be covered in a general manner without lengthy mathematical statements, but operations research is a complex specialty, and marketing managers would be well advised to employ a specialist to perform the work. Systems analysis and strategic planning are less demanding in terms of mathematical skills and are more comprehensible.

Computer Technology

The general subject of computer applications in marketing has recently become of interest to forward-thinking marketing men. Like operations research, the computer revolution has affected the marketing function less than it has other fields. Despite the widespread talk about computer-based marketing systems, generally none but the simplest of systems is utilized.

Most successful large firms have their sales run on the computer, generally as part of the accounting system, and in some instances, simple analyses are performed on the sales data. These systems have occasionally been misnamed "marketing information systems." If we consider inventory control to be a part of marketing, there are some companies that have respectable systems. But the list of companies gets very small in some of the crucial areas of marketing, such as gathering data on

- Computer performance down to a product-by-product analysis of each sales territory.
- Product end-use growth.
- Competitor market share by end-use.
- Salesman effort.

In more sophisticated areas like market simulation models, the group is reduced to a handful.

In the final chapter of this book, a total marketing system is developed in which the computer is used extensively. In this chapter, the author hopes to convince marketing managers of the necessity of such a system.

The introduction of modern management technology in marketing will cause some revolution within the marketing profession. In general, the older marketing men, who have not had the benefit of a formal education in management technology, are not particularly well equipped to design and implement the new systems. Because marketing is one field where work experience is essential, the theoretical technologist, too, is unsuited for designing marketing systems. In the short term, a dialogue will have to be developed between the marketing man and the technologist. In the long run, a new breed of marketing man should evolve who is skilled both as a technologist and as a marketing man. Since the oldest of the new breed are about 30 now, the new wave will probably begin to take over by 1975 and be fully in control by 1980. Until then, there are some companies that can establish effective communications and progress, while others will suffer through a period of rising conflict between the old and new breeds during which time little change will take place.

2

*The Systems Approach
in Practice*

Once the marketing staffing problem areas have been defined and various methods of attacking these problems have been described, it is pertinent to follow the application of the systems approach in an actual case. This case will be developed under two conditions.

The first condition is that the sales manager or system designer must deal with the current marketing system; that is, he must work with available resources, current knowledge, and existing bias and attitudes. This condition reflects the situation in which the sales manager is forced to "do something as soon as possible" about improving the marketing system. In a sense, it is an "instant cure" and is a real need in today's marketing organization, since it is not usually possible to hold everything constant while a long-range system is designed.

Having attempted to improve the system on a short-term basis, the sales manager may be concerned about improving the system on a long-term basis. Under this second condition, the sales manager and system designer are allowed to develop a better system for the future. They are given time to improve the data base, to utilize more sophisticated quantitative techniques, to analyze the behavioral factors in the buyer-seller relationship, to minimize individual bias, and to think out more thoroughly the incorporation of sales effort into marketing strategy.

The first step in attacking the marketing staffing problem is to recognize the current activity as an ongoing system. In some cases it may seem that we are glorifying a simple activity by calling it a "marketing staffing system." For example, the sales manager may have developed unwritten decision rules regarding the number of salesmen. He may add salesmen in response to a competitor, on the basis of territory geography, or when he feels that the workload is too great to handle effectively. The decision may be entirely intuitive or based on a simple criterion such as dollar revenue per sales call. No matter what the existing method, it can be described as a marketing staffing system. An in-depth analysis of this existing system is the first step toward improving the staffing decision.

Setting System Goals and Objectives

The goals and objectives of the proposed marketing staffing system must be defined before the system is constructed. In Chapter 1 it was stated that goals should be defined in terms that are meaningful, and not in trite phrases. For example, "the right number of" or "enough" salesmen is a vague criterion for a staffing system.

Our case study will focus on the determination of the optimum field sales force levels for the next four years. The criterion used in carrying out this system mission will be profitability; that is, we will continue to add salesmen if the present value profit of that investment is positive. In this calculation the discount factor will be the same as the cost of capital of the firm. Our reasoning is that the main purpose of marketing is to increase the profits of the company, and that the cost of maintaining a salesman, including salary, expenses, and overhead, can be thought of as an investment to be repaid over time. This investment is not unlike the investment in plant and equipment and should be treated as such. Of course, depreciation is not a factor in the salesman investment. However, it is important to recognize that both kinds of expense are cash outflows and that the cash outflow is justified on the anticipation of cash inflows (profits) generated in the future. Considering the investment in salesmen in this way can lead to sound investment decisions, decisions that include the time value of money.

The choice of a discount factor is somewhat debatable. It may be argued that an investment in salesmen is relatively risky, since the rewards are far from certain, and that a discount factor higher than the cost of capital should be chosen to allow for risk. However, the nature of the salesman investment is such that the cash outflow in the future is flexible. If a salesman does not generate acceptable profits, he can be shifted to a new territory or dismissed. The cash outflows for an investment in a plant are not as flexible; once a piece of equipment is purchased and installed, it is more difficult to recoup a poor investment. For this reason, the investment in salesmen is considered a low downside risk investment, the cost-of-capital discount factor is used, and a positive present value profit (however small) is accepted as the decision criterion.

Goals and subgoals. It is useful to assign a code name to the main system that is designed to achieve the prime goal. In our case study, the code name SASSAFRAS was chosen. SASSAFRAS refers to a *S*elf *A*dapting *S*ystem for determining *SA*les *F*orce *R*equirements *A*nd *S*taff levels.

The code description highlights one system characteristic essential for a successful marketing staffing system: it is "self-adapting." In Chapter 1, we recognized that good decisions depend on the adaptation of the system to the marketing environment. The object is to have SASSAFRAS adapt to the environment by means of internal operating activity. To the sales manager this means that "you don't have to start from scratch if something in the environment changes"; that "the usefulness of the system is not susceptible to environmental changes." In practical terms, if a competitor doubles its sales force, SASSAFRAS will note the change and alter the output (that is, the recommended staff level). SASSAFRAS should also continue to recommend proper sales force levels if a key person (even the sales manager) is transferred. While this type of system behavior may be regarded as "too good to be true," the strength of the system's decision-making capability is based on generating relevant data and on evaluating those data in a rigorous and specified manner. This is quite different from a system that depends on the intuition of the district manager, which is subject to many factors that are difficult to control.

After we have specified a prime system objective, it is helpful to decide upon subgoals. The subgoals can be regarded as a breakdown of the system mission into less extensive parts. In general, it is necessary to achieve subgoals in order to accomplish the prime objective successfully. In this case study, two subgoals were suggested, but other subgoals and subsystems might have been developed wherever it was beneficial to divide up the prime system into more easily workable parts.

The first subgoal involved improving, if not optimizing, the logistic operation of the salesman. Included in this logistic operation would be territory assignment and organization, call pattern and frequency, and time allocation (that is, time devoted to sales calls, waiting, travel, and office paperwork). This subgoal could be achieved in certain specific ways which will be discussed later in the framework of the subsystem SALESMAN.

The second subgoal referred to the information or data deficiencies in the field (subsystem DATA) that affected the accomplishment of the prime mission. In this case, the field districts did not have access to information on product profitability, the development of new products, national economic conditions, or the national marketing strategy of competition. Although other cases exist where some or all of these data are available, too often the information is kept at the head office and not transmitted to the field.

Analyzing the Current System

Having defined certain *desired* goals of a marketing staffing system, we may proceed to analyze the current system to determine whether these goals are being achieved. The definition of the prime goal of SASSAFRAS points to the profit maximization of the applied sales effort. It may be helpful to describe this profit maximization in other ways.

For example, we might ask whether our policy is to add salesmen until the cost of the addition equals the profit on sales generated by the additional salesman. If a company has a policy of maintaining a certain profit per salesman which is considerably in excess of costs, then it is probably *not* maximizing profitability. It is probable that the typical company either is not maximizing profits or does not know whether it is.

In our case study, the recommendation to add a salesman came from either the district manager or the sales manager. There was no formal description of the methods or criteria for the decision, and the managers generally formed their judgments on whatever information was available. The field managers had information on the territories in their district. They knew about the untapped sales potential, the mix of accounts, the relative strengths and weaknesses of their salesmen, and the local geography. But they did not have knowledge of product profitability, of national economic influences on the individual products in their line, or of the long-range schedule of new product introduction. Furthermore, they were not permitted to know the company's cost of capital. In addition to lacking important data, they were generally not aware of the modern quantitative and qualitative techniques of making good manpower decisions. Finally, they were very busy people; if the data and techniques had been made available to them, they would have been hard pressed for the time in which to develop their own marketing staffing system.

The sales manager, located at the head office, had much of the data that the field manager lacked, but he was not aware of all the details on each sales territory in every district. He was able to obtain the assistance of staff marketing analysts at the head office, who could provide forecasts of the economy, new product introductions, and product profitability, but could not tell him how to relate their information to the individual sales territory. The analysts could also develop new techniques, but the sales manager was concerned as to whether these approaches were relevant to the field manager's problems. And the sales manager, too, was a very busy man.

In effect, there were data and technique problems and no one in the sales operation with time to put the system together. The realization of these problems may have led the sales manager to suspect that the marketing staffing system was inadequate, but the situation alone was not proof that the current system was not performing properly. While final proof might have depended on adding salesmen and measuring the results, some simple calculations could convince the sales manager that the system performance could be improved.

If one assumes that it is desirable to forecast manpower requirements for the next four years, then it is reasonable to compare the field managers' forecast *manpower* needs with the forecast *sales performance* of the company. It is assumed that company sales forecasts are made at the head office and that the district sales forecasts are only part of the forecasting process. Generally, the head office will forecast sales performance on the basis of the growth of the economy, expected new competitor entries, profitability, new products, and an estimate of the district's performance.

In the case studied, when the ratio of sales revenue per salesman was calculated on the basis of field manpower recommendations and head office sales revenue forecasts, the ratio was shown to increase over the four-year period. In other words, it appeared that each salesman would become a more efficient revenue producer over the next four years. Everyone seemed happy with the prospect, but an analyst questioned the ratio, since in the last five years the ratio had steadily declined. When the president asked the marketing manager how he planned to reverse this downward trend in the ratio, everyone looked embarrassed. In this case, the simple fact was that sales and sales effort had not been related, even though no one doubted that the relationship was of key importance.

Designing a Better System

Determining system constraints. It is important to recognize the current or anticipated limitations or constraints that may affect the design of an improved system. Some of these constraints may be difficult to circumvent and may limit the performance of the system. They may be removed in the short run, or may require major changes in the company's operation or in the attitudes of key personnel. Some typical constraints on the marketing staffing systems include the following:

1. The marketing staffing system structure may be required to follow a predetermined company pattern.
2. The number of salesmen may depend on manpower requirements in other areas of the company.
3. The task of determining staff levels may be assigned to a person who is at a distance from the field sales activity.
4. The availability of information and the quality of information may be limited.
5. The kind of information to be passed on to the field managers may be restricted.

An independent system designer given the task of designing the staffing system must critically analyze the constraints. Wherever there is little opportunity to change or remove the constraints, they must be worked around.

Deciding system requirements. It is important to specify exactly what the system is to accomplish. In a typical case the system might be expected to predict sales force requirements by district and by territory for a four-year period, a prediction based, of course, on the profitability criteria of the outlined system objective. This general system requirement could then be reduced to specific requirements. For example, in order to perform the general requirement, the system would have to analyze the factors relating to salesman profitability. Therefore, it would be required to consider:

1. The sales volume by product by account by salesman.
2. The unit profitability (selling cost excluded) of each product.
3. The total sales potential in the salesman's territory.
4. The degree of efficiency with which the salesman's time is spent.
5. The salesman's personal effectiveness.
6. The bias factors at each account.
7. The response of sales to sales effort (on the basis of economic and other rational factors, to be discussed in depth in a later chapter).
8. The selling cost.

The system might also be required to allocate resources for gathering data and analyzing results. For greatest efficiency, the salesman and the district manager should estimate the bias factors at each important account, because they are closer to the source. On the other hand, head office personnel should gather and analyze data relating to economic factors used in calculating the sales/sales effort response. The availability of computers may also influence this resource allocation decision.

The system structure can also be regarded as a requirement. That is, it can be required that there be effective and relevant receptors or sensing elements in the environment, that data feedback mechanisms be specified, that decision-making capability be built in, and that effectors or action elements be operative.

Another system requirement, too often omitted in applied systems, is the organization and education of human activity to desire system change, or at least not to resist it. The marketing staffing system utilizes a high proportion of human resources (as compared with machine or software resources). The system acts primarily *on* people, and is therefore highly sensitive to human resistance. It would not be overstating the case to say that this system requirement is of primary importance in the design and implementation of a successful system.

Defining the operating environment. The effectiveness of a system depends upon its ability to make meaningful recommendations relative to the environment. In order to construct internal processes to monitor the environment and alter the system accordingly, we must define the operating environment. For example, if the sales force requirements are to be chosen for a four-year future period, the operating environment will be over at least four years, and it might be advisable to extend the operating environment to five or six years. The four-year period was selected to allow for the time delay in recruiting, hiring, training, and deploying a salesman and in the time required for the salesman to gain experience on the job.

Defining the period of the operating environment can be helpful in designing environment sensors. For example, given the four-year operating environment, if the estimated development time for a technological breakthrough in an industry were seven years, a company within that industry might monitor competitors' patent applications only casually. If the development time were two years, it would be reasonable to include a more rigorous monitoring activity. It is assumed in this illustration that the technological breakthrough would significantly influence sales of a product or service.

There will probably be changes in the company organization surrounding the marketing staffing system, and these changes should be considered changes in the operating environment. SASSAFRAS should be flexible with regard to job titles and particular faces. It is also likely that there will be changing microeconomic influences on the company's products over the four-year period.

- The demand for a product may decline until it no longer justifies continued marketing effort.
- The number of competitors may increase in certain product markets.
- The current competitors may change their sales forces.
- New products may be introduced either by the company or by its competitors.
- The cost of manufacture may increase, thereby reducing the profitability of products.

In addition to these microeconomic factors, macroeconomic factors like the condition of the national economy and the import-export situation could influence product sales. Other macroeffects, though not initially of economic origin, which could affect sales volume include legislation in the fields of welfare, health, safety, and pollution control.

The operating environment is monitored by means of receptors, which must be located in the environment to gather data of potential relevance to the system. The information obtained in this process is part of a feedback mechanism essential to the self-adapting capability of the system. Continual attention must be directed to the operating environment if SASSAFRAS is to remain a vital system over time.

Constructing the improved system. Having followed the steps of the systems approach from setting goals to defining the operating environment, the system designer is faced with the task of constructing the mechanisms of the system. In this instance we are concerned with the short-term system design. It has been assumed that the first case is one in which the system designer (who may be the sales manager) has been told to do his best with the given resources. As a first step, he may diagram the current marketing staffing system (Exhibit 2) and sketch out a revised system (Exhibit 3) that will correct the most obvious problems. The corrections may be mostly in the data flow category—and we must note that only the *flow* of the data can be altered, since the quantity and quality of data are essentially fixed. The designer is also concerned with the location of the decision-making activity, the methods of decision making, and the decision criteria. In summary, it can be stated that the designer strives to get the best information to the best decision makers, and to be certain that the decision makers have a sound basis for their decisions. The case study continues as the system designer acts to implement the marketing system.

Exhibit 2
Analysis of Current System Failure
In the Decision-Making Function

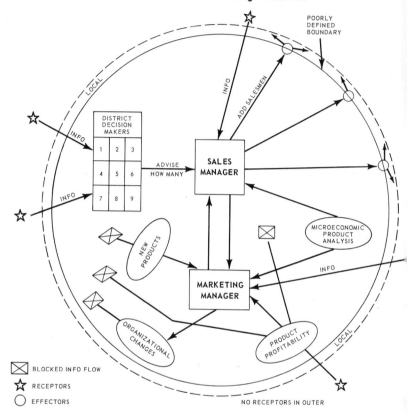

POORLY DEFINED BOUNDARY

DISTRICT DECISION MAKERS

1	2	3
4	5	6
7	8	9

INFO

ADVISE HOW MANY

SALES MANAGER

ADD SALESMEN

INFO

NEW PRODUCTS

MICROECONOMIC PRODUCT ANALYSIS

MARKETING MANAGER

INFO

ORGANIZATIONAL CHANGES

PRODUCT PROFITABILITY

LOCAL

⊠ BLOCKED INFO FLOW
☆ RECEPTORS
○ EFFECTORS

NO RECEPTORS IN OUTER

Introducing the New System

Introducing the new system into a line activity can lead to frustration and failure if the introduction is not carefully planned. A preliminary step is to define clearly the roles to be performed by the head office and field sales districts, and the proposed interactions between these two groups. In doing this, management must gain the support of all concerned personnel; the individual's resistance

44

to change must be minimized by the channeling of efforts along positive lines.

Defining the role of the head office and district. In defining the roles of the head office personnel and field personnel, the criteria to be used are resource availability and task performance. For example, the head office generally has the largest computer or data processing resource and the necessary qualified personnel to perform the data

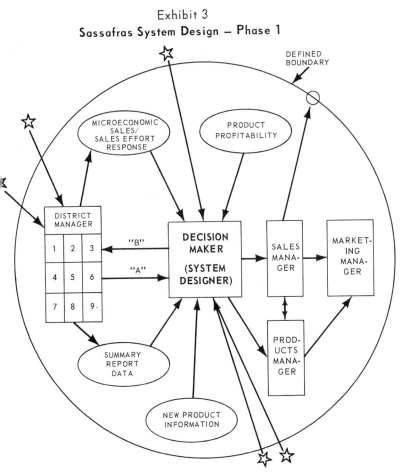

Exhibit 3
Sassafras System Design — Phase 1

processing task. It can therefore best perform roles in which a large amount of data is gathered and processed on a nationwide basis. On the other hand, the field district or regional office can best perform roles involving the gathering and analysis of detailed local information. A formal list of roles or function can be generated for each group on the basis of a careful study of the groups' specific capabilities.

In general, the head office should be charged with the following functions:

1. To gather, process, analyze, and store as a data base *national* information, such as current and forecast Gross National Product, end-use industry growth, competitor market or brand share, supply/demand ratio of particular products, new competitor products, new market entries, economic indicators, legislative changes, import-export data, foreign competition, account performance, consumer attitudes, and media effectiveness.

2. To design a staffing system to recruit, hire, and train personnel for head office and field assignments.

3. To set national sales policies, market strategies, and market plans.

4. To survey national market opportunities for new products, and to coordinate the research and development, commercial development, and sales activities for them.

5. To identify and monitor the profit generation activity of the marketing function on a national basis.

6. To coordinate nonmarketing functions that have an impact on the marketing activity.

7. To determine optimum plant, warehouse, and terminal locations, and to organize the national distribution system.
8. To develop and coordinate national advertising policies.

The field district or regional office should be charged with the following functions:

1. To gather, process, analyze, and transmit to the head office *local* information on economic prosperity and growth, product end-uses, competitor market or brand share, specific customer relationships, customer buying patterns, purchasing agent attitudes, sales territory logistics including travel time between accounts, competitor marketing strategy, competitor local advertising, and salesman time by product and by account.
2. To analyze the effect of the various influencing factors on product sales on a local basis.
3. To analyze the local market in terms of sales force requirements.
4. To work within national sales policies, market strategies, and market plans to develop local policies, strategies, and plans.
5. To survey the local market for new product opportunities.
6. To analyze the profit opportunities by account and by sales territory.
7. To evelute the local distribution capability of each competitor.
8. To analyze the need for and effectiveness of local advertising.

Head office and field interaction. The system designer should recognize those areas in which the head office and field activities must interact in order to develop an effective system, and should also be alert to areas of potential conflict. The system designer is the essential link between the two organizations in the design phase of the project; it is important that he gain the confidence of both groups so that his recommendations will be judged without bias.

The areas of interaction can be discussed in terms of the communication or information flow, the decision-making centers, and the actions taken. Information can be categorized in terms of the flow:

- From the local environment to the district.
- From the national environment to the head office.
- From the district to the head office.
- From the head office to the district.
- Within the district.
- Within the head office.

In turn, the information flow network consists of both primary transfers and feedback flows. Decision-making centers are located in both the district and the head office, and actions are taken by personnel in both groups.

Analyzing the sales district. In order to implement the new system, the system designer must visit each of the major sales districts or regions. In preparation for this on-site visit, he should gather and analyze national data, or data available at the head office, with reference to the sales staffing decision. For example, he may

1. Conduct a thorough analysis of the profitability of each of the products in the line.
2. Use the head office data bank to define the ac-

Exhibit 4
Sample District Summary

_____ DISTRICT

SALES TERRITORY	19XX PROFIT ON SALES	19XX TOTAL TERRITORY PROFIT POTENTIAL	PROFIT PENETRATION
Salesman A	14.1C	24.5C	58%
Salesman B	11.2C	45.0C	25%
Salesman C	10.0C	27.2C	37%
Salesman D	7.6C	31.7C	24%
Salesman E	6.0C	44.0C	14%
Salesman F	5.3C	24.1C	22%
Salesman G	4.2C	21.5C	19%
Salesman H	3.5C	27.5C	13%
Salesman I	1.5C	17.1C	9%
DISTRICT AVERAGE	7.2C	28.6C	25%

C = National average overhead salesman cost/year

tual sales by product and sales potential during the previous year in each district and sales territory, and determine the ratio of the two (sales penetration).

3. Combine items 1 and 2 to develop the product's, the district's, and the sales territory's profit potential, actual profit, and profit penetration.

This profit information can be expressed as a multiple of overheaded salesman's cost to obtain a measure of total salesman contribution (see Exhibit 4).

In addition, the system designer may use the head office's time-shared computer to perform regression analysis for determining the correlation between actual sales and sales effort by product over time. (A detailed explanation of this method is presented in Chapter 4.) In this manner, he can rank products by historical response to applied sales effort.

The system designer may also study available data on the relationship of product sales to other influencing variables, including

1. The relationship of national economic performance and product demand.
2. The influence of competitive products.
3. The national sales strategies of competitors.
4. The product end-use growth rates and changing technological factors that are affecting or could affect end-use sales potential.
5. The possible new market entries and their effect on supply/demand.

Before the system designer visits the district, he should ask the district manager to gather and analyze local information on sales staffing. The district manager should then be prepared to discuss local factors such as

1. Current states of all major accounts in terms of sales, potential sales, salesman/customer relationship, salesman sales strategy, and ongoing sales promotions.
2. Logistics of the district and each sales territory.
3. Individual salesman capability and ongoing salesman training or development projects.
4. Local competitor sales tactics.
5. Local competitor distribution capability.

This preparation for the on-site visit improves communication and minimizes wasted time when the system designer and district manager meet. Both parties should have a thorough understanding of the information available to them, and should recognize that each can contribute to a better staffing system.

The effectiveness of the on-site visit depends on several interpersonal factors. The status of the system designer in the organizational hierarchy of the company is generally somewhat vague in that the design assignment is temporary and of a "special assignment" nature. The system designer must therefore emphasize in his relationship with the district or regional manager that they are "on the same team" and must combine to accomplish their common task.

The effectiveness of the meeting and the continuing communication will be affected adversely if the district manager fears that the system designer is a "spy" from the head office or is trying to "run his show" in the field, or if the district manager perceives the status of the system designer as a position either subservient or overly superior to his own. To avoid these misunderstandings, senior management should initially define the purpose of the system designer and the common mission of the district manager and the system designer. In fact, a few personal phone calls from higher management to the district managers may be valuable in smoothing the way for the system designer's visit.

The system designer should also be concerned about his relationship with the salesmen. The salesman is both an essential source of information and the means by which the system will perform. Few salesmen respond favorably to a division of their sales territory to make room for an extra salesman. It is important for the system designer to emphasize that management believes that the original salesman can really put his talents to work in a smaller territory; that the system designer is there to design territories that are not too large for the salesman to cover without diluting his efforts. In this way, the system designer can win the salesman's confidence. The system designer must always be sensitive to these interpersonal relationships, or the successful implementation of the project will be jeopardized.

The conversation between the system designer and the district manager should bring out the fact that they are seeking the solution to a very complex problem. The determination of how large a sales staff is optimum and where the salesmen should be located is complicated by the numerous variables that affect the decision. When the two come to an agreement, it will probably be decided that the solution is "most likely" to be successful at that time. A continuous process of analysis, action, and feedback is necessary and the solution should tend toward an ultimate optimum, even if such a goal may never really be reached in the complex world of marketing.

Here is an example of the kind of conversation that is meaningful: the system designer describes the head office analysis of sales territories (Exhibit 4). He notes that there is a considerable variance in the profit on sales by territory (1.5C–14.1C, where C=the national average overheaded salesman cost per year), in the profit potential by territory (17.1C–45.0C), and in the percent profit penetration (9–58 percent). He suggests that Salesman A's performance is highest because his territory is manageable (small enough in potential) and allows him to concentrate his skills effectively. Now the district manager may point out that the performance of Salesman A is due to several large accounts in his territory that have been customers for many years, and that Salesmen F, G, and H have territories with the same potential as Salesman A's, but mostly with smaller accounts that are hard to sell. On the other hand, the district manager may say that Salesman A is his best salesman and would be successful in a territory with twice the potential.

The system designer then suggests that the territory potentials be made relatively equal. The district manager agrees, perhaps adding that one of the main reasons for variance in territory potential is that older salesmen are allowed to keep their good accounts and territories intact, while new salesmen are given new territories with little proven sales potential. It is probable that the older salesmen are not really covering the potential and cannot maintain an effective call schedule on all the potential customers in their territories. Also, there may be capable young salesmen who have extra time to spend in their territories.

The system designer can acquaint the district manager with the sales/sales effort data generated in the head office, and can point out those products' sales that have been "effort motivated" in the past. The district manager will be required to consider the sales effort on a product basis as well as on an account basis. The system designer can supply product profitability data to add still another dimension to the decision to add or subtract salesmen. Since the decision will be based on financial investment criteria, the factors of sales volume and potential, product profitability, profit potential, and sales effort response are of vital importance. The system designer and district manager should explore various territorial rearrangements to define areas in which the investment in a new salesman will be profitable.

One approach is to have the system designer and district manager agree on a certain new territory for an additional salesman, which will fit logistic criteria as defined by the district manager and apparently improve the district's sales effectiveness. The system designer then returns to the head office; he uses the available data base to determine the sales volume and profit potential for the new territory, both overall and by product, and determines, by means of the company's investment criteria, a minimum acceptable *sales profitability* case over a four-year period (to allow for salesman development). This sales profitability can be converted to a minimum acceptable *sales revenue* case by applying historical sales mix data. The district manager is then presented with a four-year schedule of minimum acceptable sales revenue that any new salesman whom he adds can exceed. *It is important to have the district manager be ultimately responsible for the staffing decision, because it is he who will control the salesman's performance.*

This method of determining the size of the sales staff is based on the premise that a company should continue to add salesmen until the present value profit of the investment falls below the company's cost of capital. It assumes that sales manpower is available or can be made available, and that manpower levels are not fixed or "rationed." What it does *not* do is give a rank order of new salesman investments in terms of total expected profits. It says nothing about how much sales revenue the new salesman will bring in. If the policy is followed, the sales revenue and profits per salesman will decline. However, the *total* profits generated by the sales activity will tend toward a maximum. That is the objective of this staffing system, *to maximize total profits.*

In later chapters the staffing decision will be considered in greater detail. Much of the reasoning behind this approach to sales staffing will be traced from theory to practice.

Developing a Sales Manpower Plan

When the system designer has visited the districts, framed the staffing decision, received the district manager's concurrence, and cleared the decision with higher management, he is faced with the problem of planning the manpower additions (or subtractions). This manpower plan will be influenced by the activity of many people, including the personnel department and recruiters, and must be carefully coordinated if the system is to perform satisfactorily.

The system designer may have available a pool of trained salesman candidates or no salesmen at all. In the former case, the system designer can deploy the salesmen almost immediately to improve the system. But in the latter case, assuming that a certain time period is required in which to recruit, hire, and train salesmen, all that he can do is reallocate the current sales force. In either case, he should have both a short-term and a long-term manpower plan. The ultimate objective is to have the sales force at near-optimum levels at all times.

The manpower plan can be developed in terms of a recruit–hire–train–deploy (RHTD) process in which the amount of personnel defection is measured and forecast over time. Two interesting ways of considering this RHTD process are as a quantitative physical model and as a behavioral-science exercise.

The quantitative physical model. A quantitative physical model can be developed on the principles of the flow model. This approach, diagramed in Exhibit 5, considers

Exhibit 5
Flow Model of Recruit–Hire–Train–Deploy Process

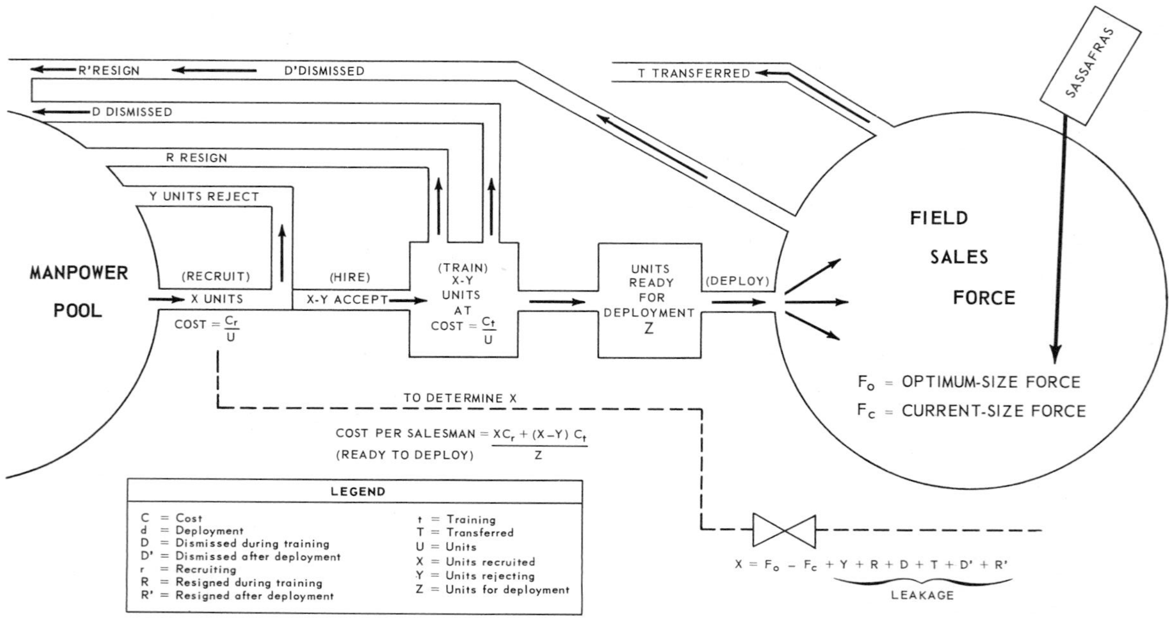

R'RESIGN
D'DISMISSED
T TRANSFERRED
SASSAFRAS
D DISMISSED
R RESIGN
Y UNITS REJECT
MANPOWER POOL
(RECRUIT)
X UNITS
COST = $\frac{C_r}{U}$
(HIRE)
X-Y ACCEPT
(TRAIN) X-Y UNITS AT COST = $\frac{C_t}{U}$
UNITS READY FOR DEPLOYMENT Z
(DEPLOY)
FIELD SALES FORCE
F_o = OPTIMUM-SIZE FORCE
F_c = CURRENT-SIZE FORCE
TO DETERMINE X
COST PER SALESMAN (READY TO DEPLOY) = $\frac{XC_r + (X-Y)\,C_t}{Z}$
$X = F_o - F_c + Y + R + D + T + D' + R'$
LEAKAGE
LEGEND
C = Cost
d = Deployment
D = Dismissed during training
D' = Dismissed after deployment
r = Recruiting
R = Resigned during training
R' = Resigned after deployment
t = Training
T = Transferred
U = Units
X = Units recruited
Y = Units rejecting
Z = Units for deployment

the salesmen as units flowing through paths. The flow model is analogous to a water system which has a source (manpower pool), a sequence of physical movements (recruiting, hiring, training) and an outlet (deployment). In addition, this system has numerous leaks (dismissals, resignations, transfers). The flow model is basically concerned with a desired output, an expected leakage in transit, and an input which is determined by adding the desired output to the expected leakage. Thus, the salesman RHTD process is characterized by a control value at the source, which is influenced by feedback processes. It is important to recognize that the key tasks are: (1) to determine the optimum or desired output, and (2) to estimate the total leakage.

When only the physical flow is considered, a high leakage factor is of no consequence. However, if we introduce a cost function, it is clear that the cost per deployable unit depends on leakage.

As illustrated in Exhibit 5, the cost per salesman ready for deployment is obtained by the following formula:

$$\text{Cost per salesman} = \frac{XC_r + (X-Y)C_t}{Z}$$

or:

$$\frac{\text{Cost per}}{\text{salesman}} = \frac{\text{Cost of recruiting all original units}}{\text{plus cost of training units accepting}}{\text{Number of units ready for deployment}}$$

The number of salesmen ready for deployment may be expressed as:

$$Z = X-Y-R-D$$

or:

$Z =$ Original units recruited *minus* units rejecting *minus* units resigning *minus* units dismissed.

Where the factors Y, R, and D represent the leakage in the RHTD process only. If the current field organization is included, the optimum manpower pool from which to recruit may be expressed as:

$$X = F_o - F_c + Y + R + D + T + D' + R'$$

or:

Manpower pool = Optimum sales force *minus* current sales force *plus* units rejecting *plus* units resigning during training *plus* units dismissed during training *plus* units transferred *plus* units dismissed after deployment *plus* units resigning after deployment.

Where Y, R, D, T, D', and R' express leakage in the total system.

The behavioral science approach. The flow model is meaningful in conceptualizing the RHTD process in terms of personnel units. However, the model ignores the human factors that influence and, in some cases, are the major determinants of the process parameters. For example, what are the factors that decide how many candidates reject the company's offer (Y) or how many resign or are dismissed (R,D)? A behavioral science approach to understanding the RHTD process focuses on these and related problems associated with human behavior.

There are five primary questions to ask with regard to the behavioral aspects of the process:

1. Why did candidates accept or reject the company's offer?
2. To what extent did the external job market contribute to the candidate's decision and to what

extent did the company's internal behavior contribute?

3. In the training phase, why did candidates resign?

4. In the training phase, why were candidates dismissed? Poor hiring decision? Inadequate training? Change in candidate's attitude or performance between the time he was hired and the time he was dismissed?

5. What has been the effect of the training phase on the remaining candidates? Are they prepared to assume the responsibility of a field assignment?

A similar set of questions can be asked to analyze the human factors that affect the current field sales force (T,D′,R′). These factors are related to the RHTD process in that they influence X, the candidates recruited.

In the next chapter the behavioral aspects of the salesman in the buyer/seller relationship will be studied with regard to their influence on the sales staffing system.

3

The Buyer and the Seller: Their Influence on the Staffing Decision

THE interaction between the salesman and the buyer is directly related to sales performance. It is important for the individual concerned with marketing staffing to determine which factors influence the buyer's purchasing decisions, and to relate the application of sales effort to these decisions. It is also important to analyze the behavior of the seller, that is, the staffing decision maker's own organization. This analysis of buyer-seller behavior is *not* normative; the analyst does not say that a type of behavior *should* take place, but that the behavior actually *does* take place.

The research that is described in the literature on the marketing function of buyer-seller behavior tends to relate to consumer buyers. On the other hand, literature directed to the industrial marketer is rarely academic and tends to focus on how-to-sell tactics. Unfortunately, it is often difficult to translate personal marketing experience from one situation to another.

The analysis of the industrial buyer should not be directed only to the individual buyer; the experienced industrial marketer recognizes that the purchasing agent's decision to buy or not to buy depends on both the individual and the organization in which he functions. This dual level of decision is one key difference between industrial and consumer buyer behavior, and is often of more importance than the legendary "greater rationality" of the industrial buyer. It also makes buyer-behavior research that is psychologically oriented difficult to relate to marketing planning.

Because the study of buyer-seller behavior is a relatively new field in industry, it is worthwhile to mention one important published work based on actual case studies. Although it is not a "canned" program that can be applied to all business situations, and should be considered research, the work is extremely valuable in illuminating this new and promising field. In this work, entitled "Models in a Behavioral Theory of the Firm,"[1] Cyert, Feigenbaum, and March analyzed the economic decision making of several firms in terms of both the market environment and the environment of the firm. Although the authors were concerned primarily with economic decision mak-

[1] R. M. Cyert, E. A. Feigenbaum, and J. G. March, "Models in a Behavioral Theory of the Firm," *Behavioral Science*, April 1959, pp. 81–95.

ing, it is important here to examine those aspects of their study that relate to marketing staffing decisions, and to describe, in particular, the influence of the internal organization on those decisions.

Analyzing Real Organizational Behavior

One procedure to be used in analyzing the behavior of a firm consists of four basic steps:

1. Determine the important decisions made by the firm.
2. Develop descriptive models of these decision processes.
3. Compare the models with actual behavior.
4. Refine and update the models by incorporating actual behavior "feedback."

Examining the behavior of a firm in this manner can lead to valuable insights. Too often, individuals make decisions on the basis of an idealized representation of the firm's behavior. For example, many companies talk in terms of a "profit maximization" goal. This goal is virtually impossible to define in terms of the concrete behavior of the firm. The possession of "perfect information" about a firm's competitors is an underlying assumption in many decision-making situations in a firm, although, in reality, the firm's knowledge is relatively imperfect. The results of decisions based on the misconception of perfect information will be disappointing.

There is much talk about long-range marketing planning and goal setting. In terms of actual behavior, however, a firm may set short-term goals in response to short-term requirements. A continuum of short-run decisions will not satisfy the requirements of a long-run plan. Even when long-term goals are set, a large firm may base its decisions on the assumption that resources are unlimited, and yet the mechanisms by which these resources are made available are often neglected or not scheduled in phase.

The existence of goal conflicts within organizations is rarely admitted, and the process by which these conflicts are resolved is rarely illuminated. Furthermore, the goals resulting from this process of conflict resolution are seldom compared with the original, theoretical goals, which have been predicated on the existence of a common goal. Too often, in real organizational behavior, individuals attempt to avoid uncertainty by choosing short-run, lower-risk decisions that are based on "loss avoidance." That is, they choose the set of alternatives that will result in no loss and low reward, rather than the set that will result in loss but eventual high reward.

Real behavior within a firm will necessarily differ from ideal or stereotyped descriptions of behavior, because decisions are made by people and not by firms. The recognition of the problem of real behavior is a key step in developing marketing systems that work. Let us examine six reflections of real behavior in marketing staffing decisions:

1. Sales performance goals may be set without regard for sales effort.
2. Sales manpower may be planned for yesterday, not tomorrow.
3. Sales effort may be expended without regard for competitor activity.
4. Sales effort may be governed by outdated principles of management.

5. Sales effort changes may be influenced by individual bias.
6. The salesman's perception of the organization may affect sales.

Setting sales performance goals without regard for sales effort. (See Exhibit 6.) It is common for organizations to develop short- and long-run sales goals without considering the role of sales effort, which is treated as a marketing cost to be "kept under control." In the annual budget, sales goals become the reflection of a bargaining process on the part of managers responsible for performance. Since they recognize the importance of achieving sales goals, they tend to set these goals below expected achievement levels to guard against the appearance of poor performance. The cost of salesmen is then treated as a cost to be held constant, or even reduced, "in order to improve profits." The fact that the achievement of sales goals is dependent upon the application of sales effort is not considered in this budgeting process. Such reasoning is all too typical in many organizations, even though it is apparent to all marketing practitioners that sales effort is essential to the marketing process. The problem arises when sales effort and sales goals are not treated as a connected cause-effect relationship in the planning-budgeting process.

It may be difficult for a participant in this organizational process to recognize that the problem exists, especially if it arises in a disguised form. For example, if the budget is set so that the amount of sales effort is appropriate for the sales goals proposed, and then the budget is challenged by a higher executive who wishes to increase profits, the management may arbitrarily reduce marketing costs and leave sales goals unchanged. The assumption

Exhibit 6

Setting Sales Performance Goals Without Regard for Sales Effort

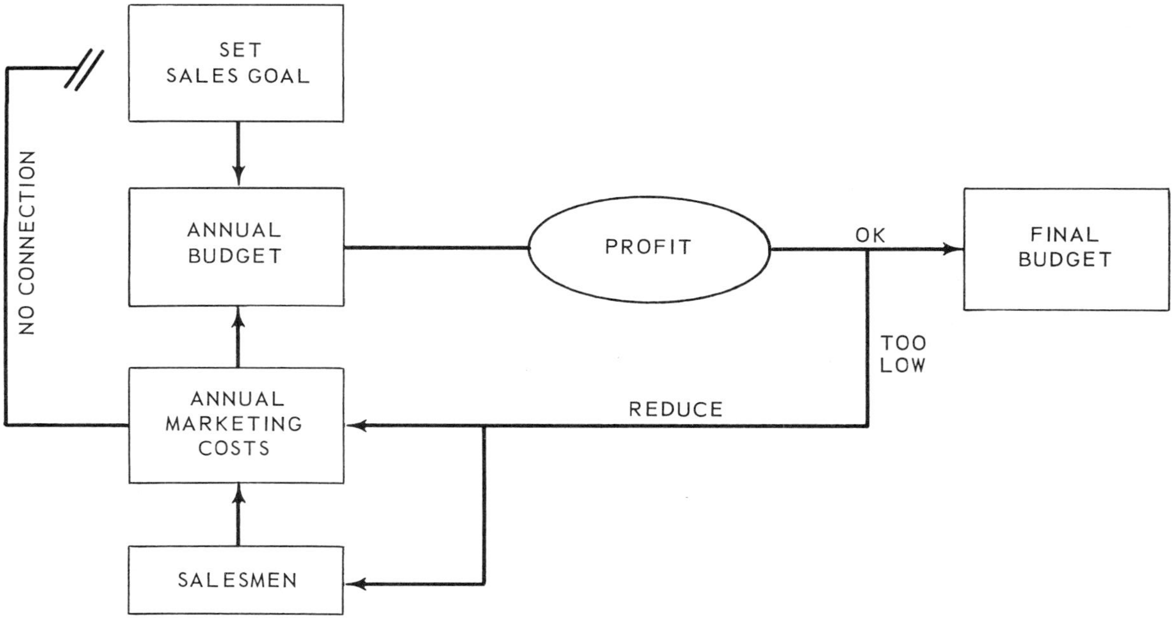

involved is not unlike the false belief that a salesman's effort can be expanded indefinitely, that he will "rise to the occasion" to sell a new product by spending more time in selling, without changing effort on the old products. Ignoring the sales/sales effort relationship in setting performance goals will generally result in the under- or nonachievement of those goals, unless enough "slack" is built into them.

Planning sales manpower for yesterday. (See Exhibit 7.) An organization often determines sales force levels by considering the past. Actually, the decision to increase the sales staff is based on the present, but by the time the salesman has been recruited, hired, trained, and deployed, the present has become the past. Thus the salesman being deployed today is relevant to a market environment of two years ago.

Expending sales effort without regard for competitor activity. (See Exhibit 8.) There are two basic classes of this behavior. The first concerns an ignorance of the competitor's sales effort alone, and the second an ignorance of the competitor's sales effort and other competitive weapons in combination. In the first situation, an organization does not know how many salesmen the competitors have, where they are located, how capable they are, how much they are paid, or how much information they control. Occasionally, the organization will try to obtain information by asking the competitor point-blank, but seeking information from a party that has the greatest reason to pass on misleading data or none at all is a dubious tactic at best. In the second situation, the organization does not realize that its sales manpower additions may be wasteful if the competition intends to reduce price. Such a situation is complex to analyze and is probably a problem with all organizations.

Exhibit 7

Planning Sales Manpower for Yesterday

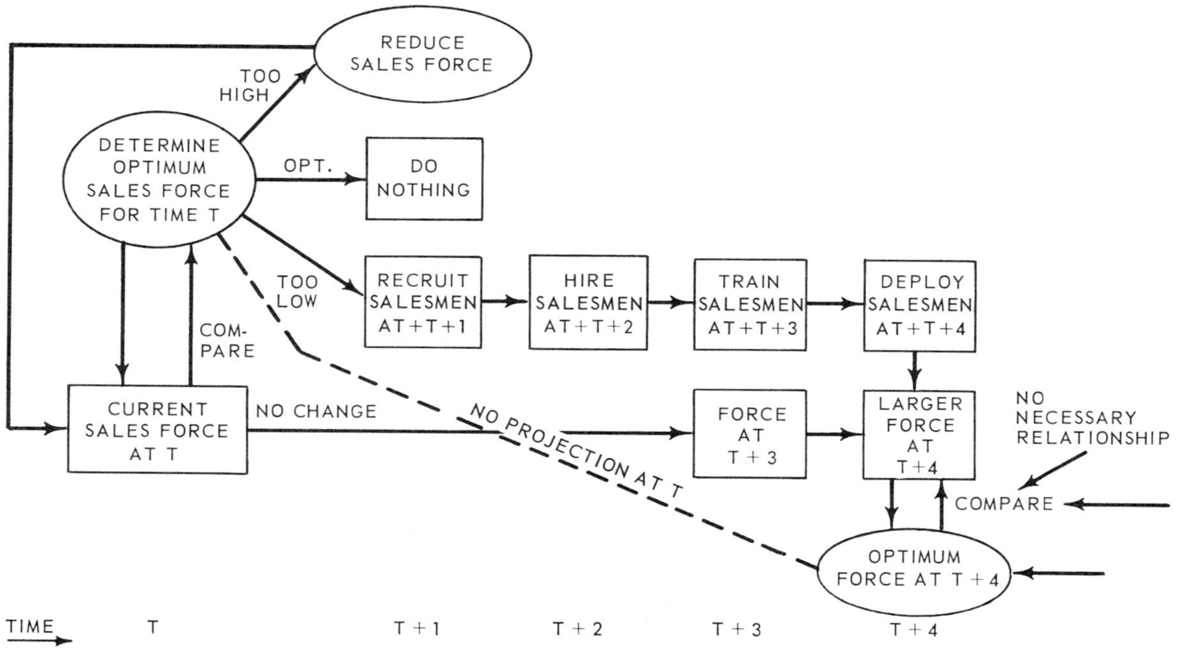

Exhibit 8
Expending Sales Effort Without Regard for Competitor Activity

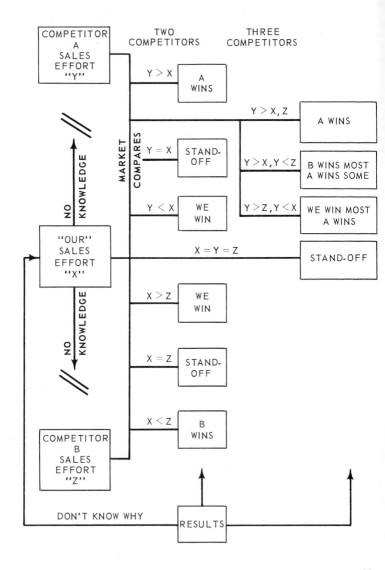

This type of behavior is often evident in new product introduction, where the number of additional salesmen needed to sell the new product is determined solely on the basis of the logistics of customer location and salesman coverage. Sales performance will be disappointing unless the behavior of the potential competition is taken into account.

Governing sales effort by outdated principles of management. (See Exhibit 9.) It is common for organizations, in rejecting the addition of salesmen, to offer the rationale that certain management principles, such as "span of control," are being violated. The result, unfortunately, is not an organizational change that will allow the management principles to be fulfilled, but a stable sales force and a static organization. The analysis does not focus on the opportunity lost by not adding the salesman or the cost of increasing the number of managers. In addition, the "principles" are not scrutinized to determine their real value.

Changing sales effort according to individual bias. (See Exhibit 10.) In organizations where the decision to change sales effort rests on the opinion of an individual, rather than on quantitative or other rational grounds, the decision may be subject to considerable bias. The sales manager may attempt to "build an empire" by adding salesmen without appraising the value of the addition. On the other hand, the district manager may not wish to accept the increased burden of managing additional salesmen in his district.

Changing sales effort according to the salesman's perception of the organization. (See Exhibit 11.) Previously, we have discussed the behavior of the management. The salesman, as part of the organization, can also have a direct effect on sales effort, and should be considered as part

Exhibit 9

Governing Sales Effort by Outdated Principles of Management

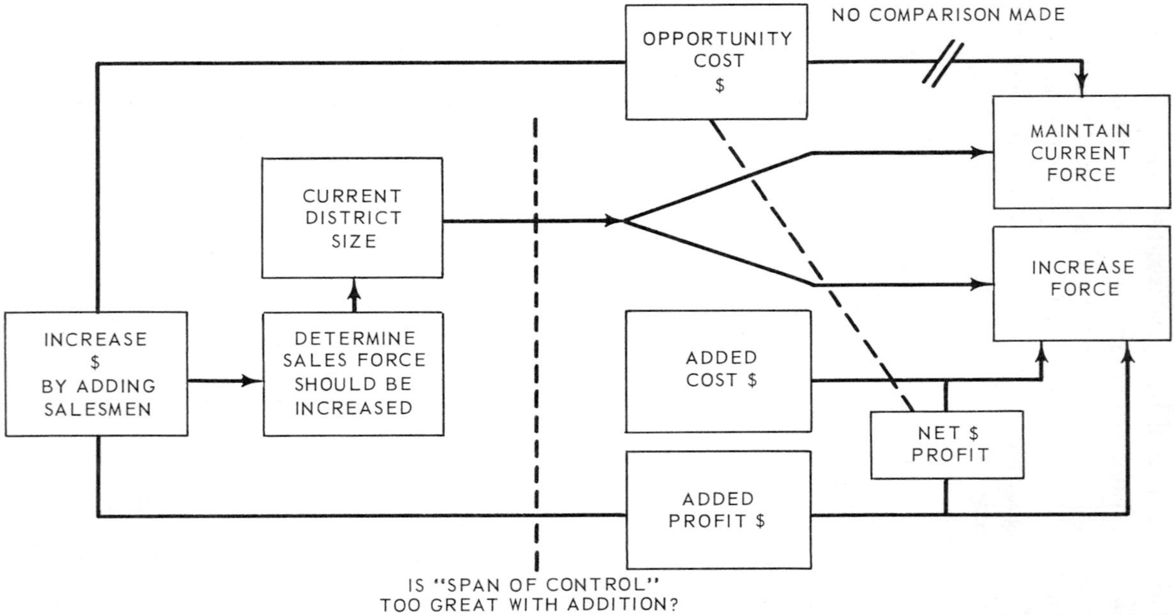

NO COMPARISON MADE

MAINTAIN CURRENT FORCE

INCREASE FORCE

NET $ PROFIT

OPPORTUNITY COST $

ADDED COST $

ADDED PROFIT $

CURRENT DISTRICT SIZE

DETERMINE SALES FORCE SHOULD BE INCREASED

INCREASE $ BY ADDING SALESMEN

IS "SPAN OF CONTROL" TOO GREAT WITH ADDITION?

Exhibit 10

Changing Sales Effort According to Individual Bias

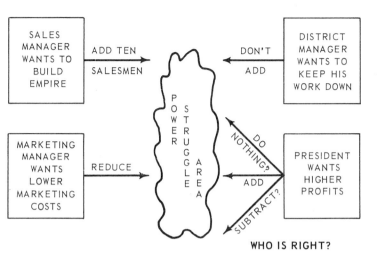

WHO IS RIGHT?

of the behavioral aspects of the organization. If the sales-man perceives that his status in the organization is not as high as he feels it should be, his sales effort will decline or become less effective; if other salesmen share his feeling, the turnover rate will probably increase. Similar effects will result when the salesman does not feel that his career is being planned, that future promotions will be based on merit, or that his remuneration is reasonable. It should always be remembered that management's intentions and policies may be incorrectly perceived by the salesman, and that it is the salesman's *perception* of the organization that is the key to his performance.

Analyzing Buyer Behavior

The activities of the seller organization must be related

Exhibit 11
Changing Sales Effort According to the
Salesman's Perception of the Organization

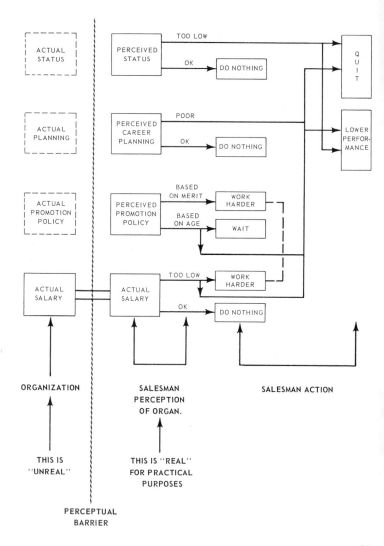

to the actual behavior of the buyer. In this case, too, it should be recognized that there may be a significant difference between theoretical, idealistic, or normative buyer behavior and actual buyer behavior. Keying the selling effort to a buyer behavior that is nonexistent will result in poor sales performance or an inefficient use of valuable salesman resources.

Sales performance is the result of a complex interaction that encompasses the behavior of the buyer and seller in a dynamic marketplace. In the next section of this chapter, the behavior of the industrial buyer will be analyzed, and the same analytic process may be used for the consumer-buyer. In both cases it is important to define the influences of the organization (firm or family) on the buyer's decision.

The individual buyer rarely, if ever, acts as an independent decision maker. His decision to buy is influenced by the management hierarchy, various department recommendations, historical purchase patterns, and intercompany relations, in addition to the obvious "need to buy." In dealing with an oligopolistic market, we are interested in *what firm* the buyer selects rather than *how much* he buys; we can assume that production scheduling and inventory constraints guide the buyer in deciding how much to buy. Also, we are interested in *what product* the buyer buys in interproduct competition when a need has been established. Every attempt will be made to reflect the typical industrial buyer in a real situation. In Exhibit 12 we have diagramed the various influences on the buyer's decision. The seven basic influences are:

1. The engineering, technical, and manufacturing departments.
2. The scheduling or receiving department.

Exhibit 12
Influences on Industrial Purchasing Decisions

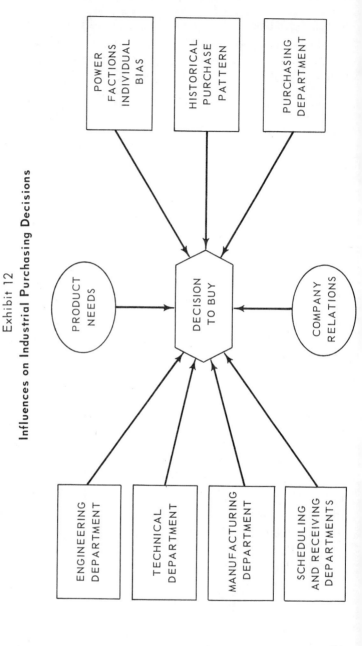

Exhibit 13

The Engineering, Technical, and Manufacturing Departments
Influence the Buying Decision

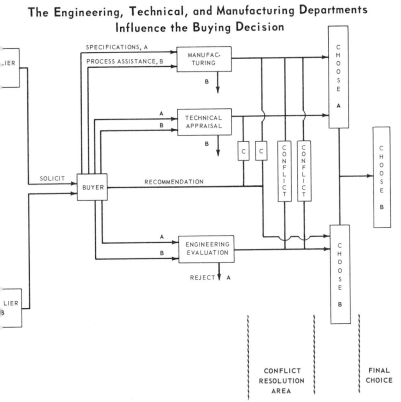

3. Power factions and individual bias.
4. Historical purchase patterns.
5. Company relations.
6. Product needs.
7. The purchasing department.

The engineering, technical, and manufacturing departments. (See Exhibit 13.) The engineering department may influence the buyer by recommending a specific supplier, particularly when the product used by the company requires the supplier's technical assistance or is so tech-

Exhibit 14

The Scheduling or Receiving Department Influences the Buying Decision

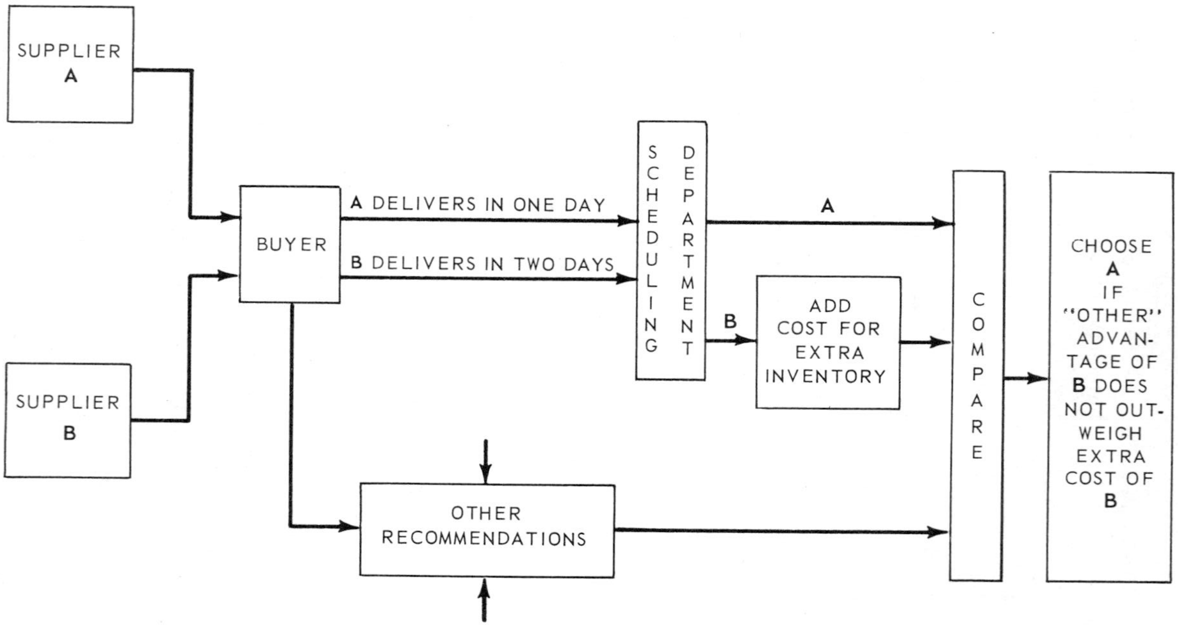

nologically complex that only the engineering personnel are capable of judging its true value. Other technically oriented departments may affect the decision process for similar reasons. Manufacturing personnel will often influence the decision in cases where the product's specifications are critical to its performance in the manufacturing process. Suppliers may offer to assist the manufacturing department in using the product to advantage or even in improving the overall manufacturing process only part of which is related to the product in question.

The scheduling or receiving department. (See Exhibit 14.) The departments in the buyer's organization that are responsible for scheduling product inputs, inventories, and outputs to the manufacturing operation may be a deciding influence in selecting a supplier. The supplier that cannot deliver a product in a reliable manner, on time and on specification, is a definite liability to the buyer's organization. If the supplier can deliver in a short period of time, the buyer can maintain lower inventories and invest less capital in storage and warehousing facilities. In many instances, the reliable supplier is considered an extension of the buyer's organization.

Power factions and individual bias. (See Exhibit 15.) The purchasing representative of an organization operates within the power structure and hierarchy of his own company. The buyer who contacts the supplier may have to report to several bosses within the purchasing organization, who in turn have to report to higher managers in the company. Thus the buyer's decision may be determined by the will of a higher authority and in certain instances this impressed decision may be based on irrational factors.

Historical purchase pattern. (See Exhibit 16.) It is common for buyers to repeat purchasing patterns established in the past. Whether their reluctance to change

Exhibit 15

Individual Power Factions and Bias Influence the Buying Decision

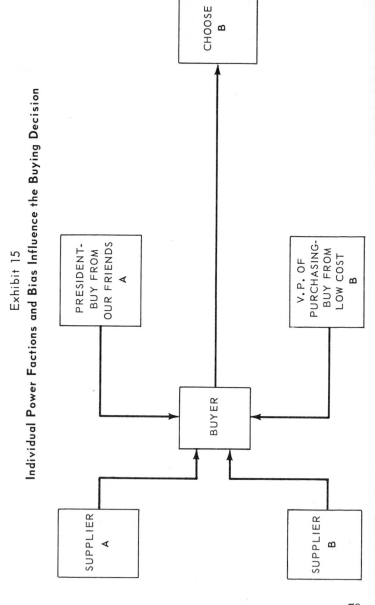

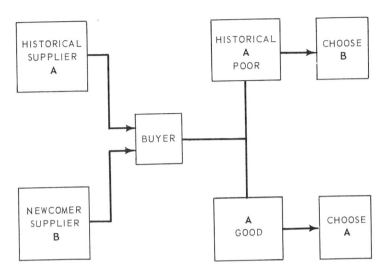

suppliers is called inertia, laziness, or maintenance of continuity, the better supplier may have difficulty in overcoming it. If the traditional supplier has been successful, the buyer may decide to keep the supplier whose abilities are proven rather than speculate on a newcomer. On the other hand, if the old supplier has a poor record, the buyer may feel that "any other company would be better." It is very difficult to displace a well-liked supplier and very simple to oust a disliked one.

Company relations. (See Exhibit 17.) A buyer may select a supplier for one product because the buyer's company sells other products to the seller's company, or because a competitive supplier competes with the buyer's company in other trade areas. Legal provisions discour-

Exhibit 17
Company Relations Influence the Buying Decision

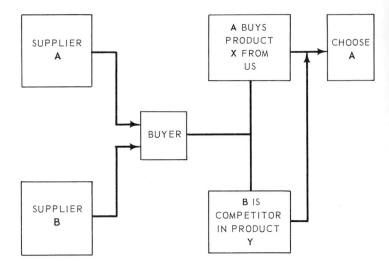

age written agreements to establish formal trade positions that reduce competition. However, there is no law against swinging an even decision to a friendly supplier, as opposed to a competing one.

Product needs. (See Exhibit 18.) The need for a product is an essential ingredient in the buying decision. This need, however, may result from the supplier's establishing the need or may be a latent need that the supplier uncovers. Once established by the supplier, the need becomes an influencing factor from the buyer's standpoint.

The purchasing department. (See Exhibit 19.) Even though there are many other influences within the buyer's organization, the individual purchasing agent is a very important factor in the buying decision. In many companies, the purchasing agent is the only contact with the

Exhibit 18
Product Needs Influence the Buying Decision

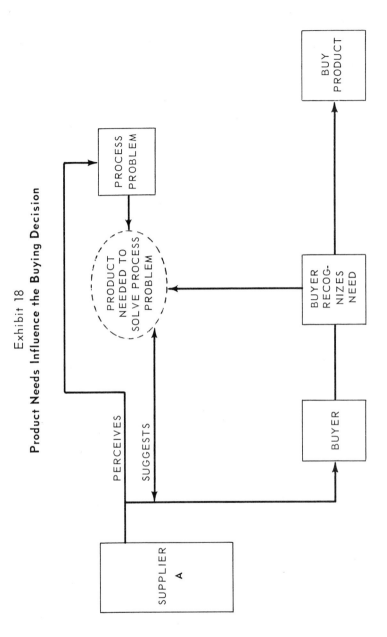

Exhibit 19

The Purchasing Department Influences the Buying Decision

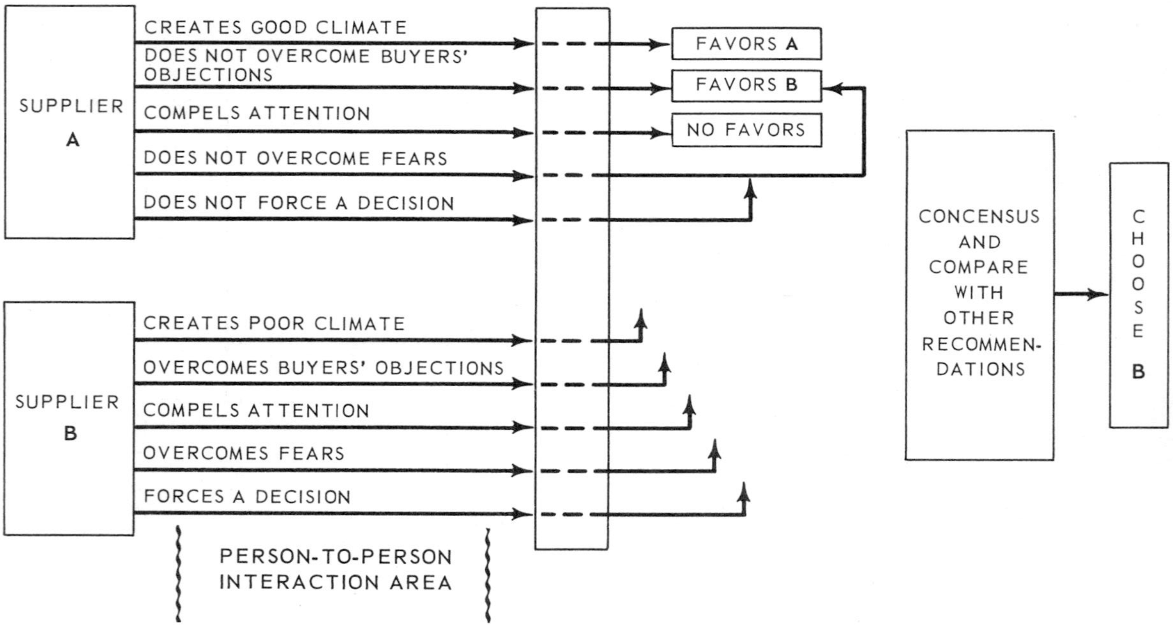

seller; in others, all contacts are made through him and with his permission.

The mix of personalities in discussions between the purchasing agent and the salesman may have a marked influence on the buying decision. Practitioners of marketing have devoted a great deal of effort to improving the effectiveness of the salesman by training him to react to the personality of the buyer. Conversely, the buyer is often educated in the psychological tactics of the salesman so that he can develop a high degree of buyer objectivity in evaluating the supplier's strengths and weaknesses.

It is incorrect to regard the personal interaction of buyer and seller as a factor of some past era when marketing was less rational and less scientific. In truth, the increased complexity of the marketplace, in which there are so many more competitors and salesmen, has made interpersonal relationships more and not less important. The seller must establish a unique identity that will distinguish him from the crowds of faces that daily besiege the buyer; developing a rapport with the buyer is one way of doing this. It has been suggested that, in the future, personal contact of seller and buyer will be superseded by intercomputer communication, including analysis of bids. However, the efforts by competitors to equalize strengths and weaknesses, as well as the limitations on bid evaluation, will tend to maintain the importance of personal contact. Sales effort and personal friendship are not the most powerful of competitive weapons, but they do become very important when other weapons have been neutralized.

These verbal descriptions of how the buyer and seller are influenced by their organizations can be enhanced by developing a process model of the behavioral patterns. The decision process model clarifies the decision possibilities and their relevant bases, and can then be translated into a computer program. The use of a computer allows the decisions to be evaluated systematically in terms of the parameters that influence them.

Analyzing Buyer-Seller Interaction

We have discussed the organizational influences on the buyer-seller relationship. The remaining area of interest is the marketplace where buyer and seller interact. The behavior of the industrial buyer in the marketplace can be defined in terms of several decisions. The buyer decides to shop, decides to purchase, and decides to buy from a particular supplier or set of suppliers.

Decision to shop. The initial decision that the industrial buyer must make is to shop or to make himself available for sales solicitation. In part, this decision is a result of conditions and activities within the buyer's organization. As we have observed, the need for the product can be established either through hierarchial dictate within the buyer's organization or by a potential supplier who assists in creating or pointing out a need from his position in the marketplace. Industrial advertising is one aspect of the supplier-formed perception of need that can influence the buyer in his decision to shop. Other factors within the buyer's organization also influence this decision, for example, the availability of financial resources.

Decision to purchase. The buyer's decision to purchase is influenced by the product price, the amount and effectiveness of the sales effort, the product quality, the distribution facilities, the availability of technical support supplied by the seller, and the value of the product to the buyer. It is important to keep the decision to purchase and the choice of supplier as separate decisions, even though they are related. For example, if all suppliers quoted the same price (all other factors being equal), the decision to purchase would be in terms of the price level rather than a specific supplier. The decision to purchase may result from the buyer's evaluation of one factor or many, depending on the buyer's judgment.

Decision to purchase from a particular supplier. The decision to purchase from a particular supplier is the decision in which operating marketing personnel are most interested. The buyer's interest in a particular supplier is in direct proportion to the value that he obtains from that supplier as compared with another supplier or any supplier. The supplier is concerned only with obtaining the business, and, in fact, would prefer to win the business by creating the least differential advantage. Considering price only, the buyer would be pleased to receive one very low price, while the winning supplier would like to shade the price of his nearest competitor only slightly. Under conditions in which a very low price will not gain more business than a shaded price, the supplier who bids too low obviously receives less profit and the buyer potentially more.

The behavior of the buyer in the decision to select a supplier can be regarded as a response to a dynamic market in which competitors use weapons to establish a competitive difference. Chapter 6 presents a detailed study of this competitive "game." In brief, the buyer acts to evaluate suppliers on the basis of several parameters, including price, sales effort, technical support, distribution capability, quality, image, and reliability. The sellers may choose to compete on an intraweapon basis, such as price versus price, or on an interweapon basis, such as price versus sales effort. The competitive game takes place over time in a dynamic fashion. When the buyer enters the market, the competing suppliers will either specially adapt their behavior to the entering buyer or categorize him in terms of existing buyers, depending on the degree of buyer uniqueness and the potential value of the buyer's business to the seller. In a sense, each buyer is unique and must be treated as such by the seller. But the degree of buyer uniqueness can be overestimated, and it is important for sellers to examine aggregate buyer behavior in developing general marketing strategies.

Some marketing men believe that if a supplier has a good relationship with a particular buyer, then the buyer will purchase many products from the supplier. This approach is account- or buyer-oriented in that the differences in economic characteristics of the products are regarded as less important. Others feel that the economic characteristics of a product will be more related to the buying decision than will the relationship of the buyer and supplier. This approach is product-oriented. The difference of opinion hinges on the value of the buyer-seller relationship and the importance of certain economic product characteristics. In a typical case, the seller may have to make a decision about increasing sales effort. The account-oriented marketer will expect good results from this action, while the product-oriented marketer will say that the results depend on whether the particular product will be influenced by sales effort. If, for example, the product is in excess supply, the product-oriented marketer will suggest that the results will be disappointing.

This argument is a crucial one and should be debated at length in seller organizations. Certainly, there is no reason why both positions cannot be considered together and the potential results projected by evaluating both account and product effects.

This concludes the description of the behavioral approach to the buyer-seller relationship and the marketing staffing decision. In many ways, it may appear to be an obvious approach, since the intelligent manager or even the alert new employee can easily perceive discrepancies between the purported and actual behavior of the firm. But even when these discrepancies are recognized, they are rarely written down in a critical manner and analyzed with an eye to altering undesirable behavior. Rather than go against the political/hierarchial grain of the organization, most individuals would prefer to remain silent and suffer the frustrations of working with an entity that purports to be one thing but is actually another.

4

Analyzing Sales Effort in Quantitative Terms

In the previous chapter the marketing staffing decision was analyzed in terms of a description of actual behavior. No attempt was made to quantify the behavioral models. In this chapter the emphasis will be on quantifying actual behavior or, when actual behavior is unknown, hypothetical behavior. The quantifying process improves decision making and allows the use of mathematically based calculators such as the computer. The system then becomes easier to comprehend, and the analyst and manager can communicate better with each other by working with the universal language of mathematics.

Up to now, unfortunately, operations research and the computer have not been used extensively in the field of marketing. One of the reasons for this is that marketing systems depend on numerous variables that are difficult to quantify because of their high human resource content, which forms what can be described as a complex environment. In dealing with the complex marketing environment, researchers have tended either to oversimplify the system or to develop a very complex mathematical approach. The oversimplified model is quickly recognized by the marketing manager as being too simple to help him; the complex approach is mathematically "over his head." Again, the immediate problem is that there are few individuals who are competent both as operations researchers and as marketing analysts.

At present, there are few "canned" quantitative approaches that can be easily applied throughout the wide range of marketing activity. It is necessary to sift through the research, to distill out the essence of the approaches, and to adapt an approach to the particular marketing system. Fortunately, some of the useful techniques are not mathematically complicated. At this stage, the focus is on combining quantitative approaches with the intuitive judgment of experienced marketing personnel in order to clarify the marketing activity with regard to the staffing decision.

Sales Response to Sales Effort

One of the prime considerations in determining how many salesmen should be deployed in the field is the sales response to sales effort, that is, the relationship between the salesman's effort (including solicitation time and the effectiveness of the salesman in using that time) and the sales generated as a direct result of that sales effort. We recognize, of course, that sales effort is only one of the many factors that influences sales, and that the influence of the other factors (such as price and advertising) varies from account to account and from product to product. We are interested in the aggregate relationship of sales effort to sales, with the influences of all the other factors included. Thus if one product in a line is known to sell on price alone, we can assume that the sales of that product will not be greatly affected by changes in sales effort. In other words, we are not saying that sales effort is all-important; we are trying to find out how important it is.

One way of considering the sales response to sales effort is to construct a graph with sales on the Y-axis and sales effort on the X-axis. It is useful to examine the percent change in sales for a given percent change in sales effort. This graph can be generated from actual, historical data (if available) or from intuition on a hypothetical basis. The hypothetical approach will be discussed first, because it is likely that data on sales effort by product over an extended time period are not available in the typical firm. By using intuitive reasoning, the marketing manager or marketing analyst chooses a product and plots the sales response curve.

To simplify the analysis, let us assume that the product is a mature product and not a new one. What should the curve look like? To begin with, would the curve bisect the origin? That is, if the percent change in sales effort were zero (effort constant), would the percent change in sales be zero also? Or would sales grow or decline at some rate because of other factors? Next, we pick an arbitrary percent change in sales effort, say 5 percent. What would the percent change in sales be? We continue in this manner until several points are plotted, and then draw a curve through the points. After the first attempt it will become evident that constructing this sales response curve from

Exhibit 20
Sales Response Models

intuition is far from easy. And yet doesn't plotting such a curve really express an essential aspect of managing sales effort?

Before we attempt to construct a sales response curve to reflect a real product, we may find it helpful to consider the curve in general. The shape of the curve could be a straight line or a power or exponential model (Exhibit 20). Generally speaking, a good hypothetical curve would combine a linear and exponential curve to look somewhat like an S (Exhibit 21). In this manner, the

Exhibit 21
Hypothetical Total Response Curve

total product life cycle is considered from introduction as a new product through a leveling-off or saturation phase; the inevitable decline is not taken into account. It is reasoned that when a new product is introduced, the sales response to sales effort is low, because the potential buyers have to learn about the product, determine its value to them, and so on. After a time, as the initial problems are overcome, the sales begin to increase in proportion to the applied sales effort. A period of maturity follows, and then

92

an eventual leveling off as the market becomes saturated with the product.

Having developed this general response curve, we should be able to determine where each of a firm's major products falls on the curve by categorizing it as a new, mature, or saturated product. Some obvious questions can be asked of the marketing manager at this point:

1. New Products. Do long-term sales and profit expectations justify the initial expenditure of a good deal of sales effort (sales cost) without much of a sales response?

2. Mature Products. Are you applying enough sales effort on mature products, which return a substantial sales response to sales effort?

3. Saturated Products. Are you spending too much sales effort on saturated products, where the sales response is poor and will get worse in the future?

The use of hypothetical models is necessary when adequate data on sales and sales effort are not available. However, the use of actual data is a great help in answering some of the difficult questions concerning the shape of the sales response curve. The author was fortunate enough to have actual data to work with in his case study, and hopes that the study will emphasize the value of having such data.

Single-product sales/effort response. The development of an actual sales/effort response curve is dependent on a relevant data base. Our case study focused on the time spent by the salesman in selling the product to the customer. The salesman recorded the actual time spent in direct confrontation with the purchasing representative, and these data were then modified by the salesman to reflect the relative "intensity" of the time spent. For example, if the salesman and purchasing agent talked for 55 minutes on golf and 5 minutes on the product, that hour was considered of lower intensity than an hour in which the salesman delivered a sales pitch on the reasons why the customer should buy the product. The data were collected weekly from the salesman and quarterly from the field districts, and the effort expended was reduced to a percentage of total district effort applied. These data were available for a five-year period.

Because the product was an old product, and because the known market potential was considerably lower than the actual market potential (obtained from government sources), it was determined that the sales/effort response was in neither an introductory nor a saturation phase. In other words, there existed a certain unknown sales potential that could be penetrated if known; even though the known product market appeared to be saturated, the real market (as represented by the government statistics) was not.

Regression analysis. The data were stated in terms of percent change in "direct" sales for the product in each of the sales districts versus percent change in sales effort, both over a specified period of time. "Direct" sales referred to sales to direct consumers rather than to distributors, and were modified to eliminate unusually large buying accounts that would distort the sales/effort relationship. A typical case was the annual percent change in direct sales versus the annual percent change in sales effort for a specific district. The longer time period was chosen to smooth out seasonality factors and other short-term disturbances.

The data were plotted on a chart in which the percent change in sales was on the Y-axis, and the percent change in sales effort was on the X-axis. In order to determine the most representative sales/effort response curve, a statistical technique known as regression analysis was used. By this mathematical method, a straight line was "fitted" to the data. (See Exhibit 22.) The equation of the straight line in terms of the parameters was:

Percent change in sales = .696 percent change
in effort + 1.365 percent

By use of the regression line, it is possible to determine the average percent change in sales for a given percent change in effort. For example, if effort were increased by 10 percent on Product A (that is, if the district increased effort from 10 percent of the total district effort to 11 percent), the district manager would expect a 7.3 percent change in sales *on the average*. This relationship is a historical one, since it is based on past data. It is for the marketing analyst to determine whether that relationship will hold true in the future—and it is the future, after all, that is most important for the marketing manager. Understanding the past is one approach to improving future predictions.

Regression analysis gives other interesting parameters that can be meaningful to the marketing manager. The coefficient of determination, for example, shows *how much better* one can predict the percent change in sales by considering the percent change in effort. In the example of Product A, it could be estimated that the variance of the percent change in direct product sales corresponding to a given percent change in effort allocated was about 33 percent less than the variance of the percent change in sales when effort was disregarded. This would indicate that other factors were involved in some of the variance in

Exhibit 22
Regression Analysis – Product "A"

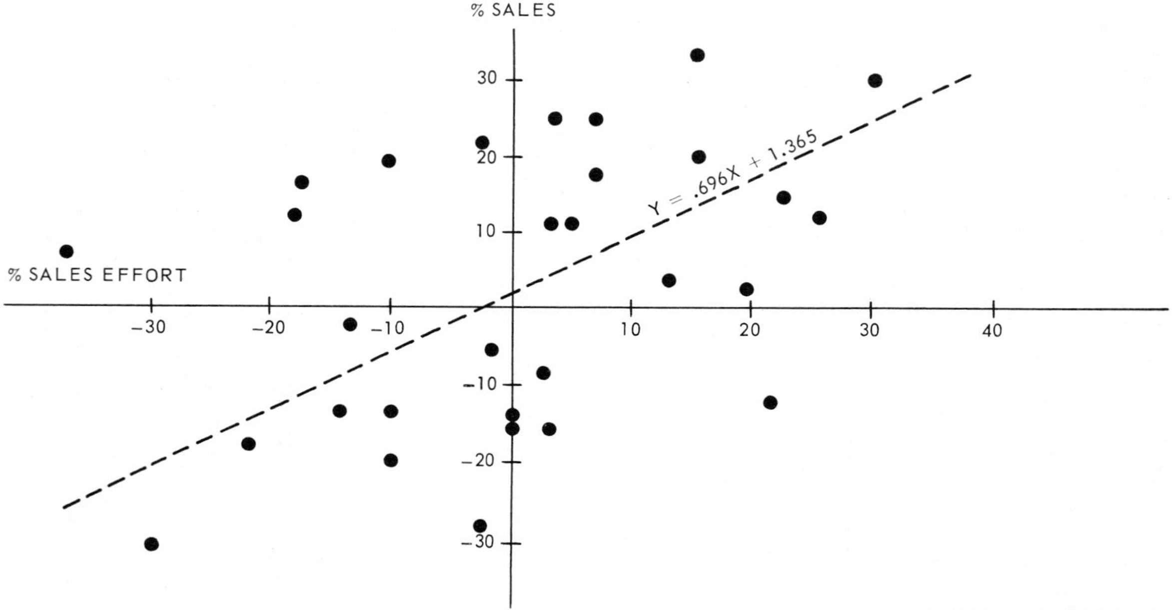

% SALES

% SALES EFFORT

$Y = .696X + 1.365$

sales. Multiple regression analysis can be used to rank factors by their relative influence on variance. For example:

- Price   35%
- Effort   33%
- Advertising   20%
- Technical support   5%
- Unknown factors   7%

A complete explanation of regression analysis can be found in most statistics texts. It should be noted that regression analysis measures correlation only; it does not prove a causal relationship. The marketing analyst must determine intuitively whether there is a causal relationship.

Multiproduct sales/effort response. The single Product A was used to illustrate the regression analysis technique. Few companies have only one product, however. Most marketing managers must be concerned with applying sales effort to many products.

In a typical case studied by the author, the product line contained several hundred products. However, when the effort expended was analyzed in depth, it was evident that 98 percent of the effort was applied to 34 products. Moreover, 12 products represented 76 percent of the total effort applied. Although it was possible to perform linear regression analysis on 34 products, the focus was on the 12 key products. The linear regression for the products (Exhibit 23) showed the response functions to be radically different. This analysis revealed that many of the products that received a large percentage of the company's sales effort had a poor response to sales effort. In

Exhibit 23
Multiproduct Regression Analysis

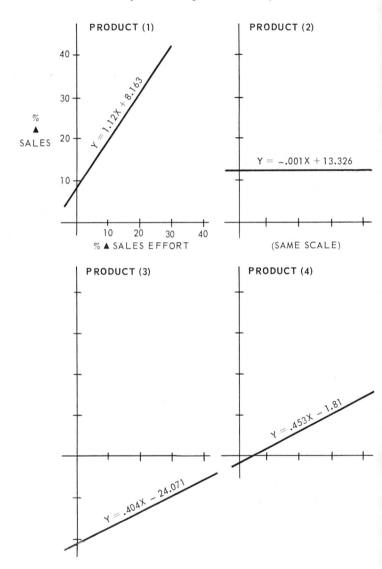

PRODUCT (1)

$Y = 1.12X + 8.163$

% ▲ SALES

% ▲ SALES EFFORT

PRODUCT (2)

$Y = -.001X + 13.326$

(SAME SCALE)

PRODUCT (3)

$Y = .404X - 24.071$

PRODUCT (4)

$Y = .453X - 1.81$

Exhibit 23 (Continued)

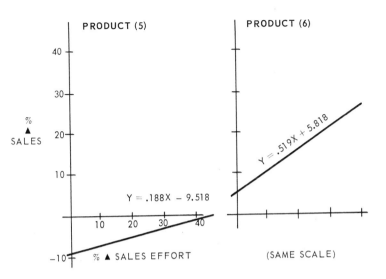

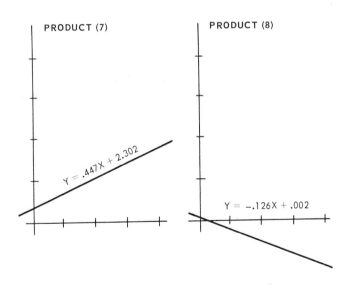

Exhibit 23 (Concluded)

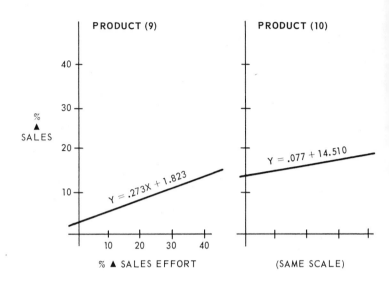

PRODUCT (9)

PRODUCT (10)

% ▲ SALES

Y = .273X + 1.823

Y = .077 + 14.510

% ▲ SALES EFFORT

(SAME SCALE)

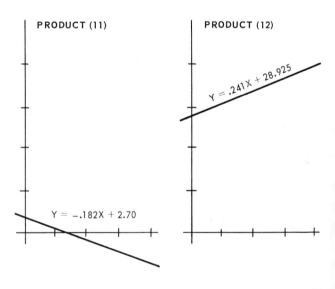

PRODUCT (11)

PRODUCT (12)

Y = −.182X + 2.70

Y = .241X + 28.925

fact, sales effort was being wasted, with two resulting losses:

- The dollars expended to sell the product.
- The dollars of profit that could have been obtained by reallocating effort to high response products.

Marketing management was astounded; it is very likely that the managers of other companies would find such an analysis equally revealing.

In the design of the SASSAFRAS Phase 1, the system designer transferred the sales/effort response information to the district managers to permit them to adjust the product mix of the sales territories in terms of the expected response to applied effort. Product profitability data were also transmitted so that a trade-off could be made between profitability and effort response.

The development of multiproduct historical regression data is the key to the marketing management's ability to manage sales effort in the pursuit of profit goals. In Chapter 5, all the economic factors that influence sales and account for the variance in response functions will be discussed.

New product introduction. There are two interesting phases of new product introduction with regard to sales effort. First, it is essential to determine how much sales effort is required to market a new product "successfully." Second, it is important to predict and measure the effect of the new product sales effort on effort applied to older products. If we assume that the new product to be introduced is not radically different from other products marketed by the company in the past, the following approach may be a valuable guide:

1. Assuming that ten-year sales volume goals can be set, estimate the sales volume level in year one that could be achieved for a specified amount of sales effort. (This first-year figure should disregard introductory-phase marketing inefficiencies.)
2. Select the sales volume goal at the end of ten years and determine the percent-per-year, compounded sales-volume growth rate.
3. Examine historical sales/effort regression data for an old product that would be considered similar to the new product in effort response characteristics.
4. Determine the percent change in effort per year required to obtain the desired percent change in sales volume per year over the ten-year period.
5. Translate the compounded annual effort growth rate in terms of sales manpower required in each project year.
6. Modify the manpower figures to account for expected differences between the new product's sales/effort response and that of the old product.

In the case studied, the sales and sales effort curves appeared as in Exhibit 24, with effort preceding sales buildup by approximately nine months. In examining these curves, one might ask, "Would it be better to add effort early or to add effort proportionally over the project life?" Because of the time value of money, the trade-off in this analysis is between the increased value of a faster sales-profit buildup and the increased cost of sales manpower. In general, it is more profitable to apply effort early.

If new salesmen are hired for the specific purpose of selling the new product, and no effort is siphoned away

Exhibit 24
Sales/Sales Effort Curve for a New Product

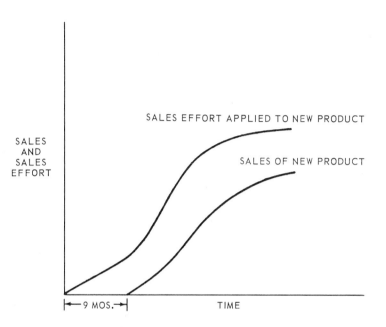

SALES EFFORT APPLIED TO NEW PRODUCT

SALES
AND
SALES
EFFORT

SALES OF NEW PRODUCT

|← 9 MOS. →| TIME

from the old products, the effect on the old products of introducing the new product is negligible. In the typical commercial situation, the sales effort is expected to come both from some new salesmen and from the increased efforts of the current field sales force, but the latter, in many cases, will be the only available source of effort. In these cases, the new product will have a tremendous effect. Generally, the assumption that the field force will "rise to the occasion" and put in extra time to sell the new product is false. In effect, the sales force will spend less time selling the old product in direct proportion to the time spent on the new product. It is important to calculate the financial effect of this shift in sales effort.

In a typical case, the introduction of a new product may use up 1 percent of the total effort in year one, 2.5 percent in year two, and 4 percent in year three. Total out-of-pocket costs for the salesmen are $25,000, $50,000 and $85,000, respectively, in the three years. Lost profits on missed sales of the old products due to the siphoning off of this effort amount to about one million dollars. The sales manager never sees the million-dollar loss, because it is in essence an opportunity cost.

It is important to recognize those situations in which the effort applied to a new product will *not* affect the effort applied to old products. As illustrated in Exhibit 25, there are four basic cases:

1. Manpower is expanded in proportion to new product requirements.
2. Manpower is constant; the effort applied to the new product is traded off against a failing product's effort decline.
3. Manpower is constant; the effort applied to the new product is traded off against effort declines on other established products.
4. Manpower is constant; the effort applied to the new product is traded off against the *net* decline in effort on other established products.

The complexity of the problem of determining the quantitative effect of effort siphoning becomes apparent when we consider the historical applied effort on *all* the old products, which often amount to a large number. (See Exhibit 26.) The question then is, "Which products acted in a causal fashion, and which products showed the results?" It is possible that the effort applied to new products and to failing products was a causal factor on the other prod-

Exhibit 25
Cases in Which Effort Applied to
A New Product Will Not Affect Effort on Old Products

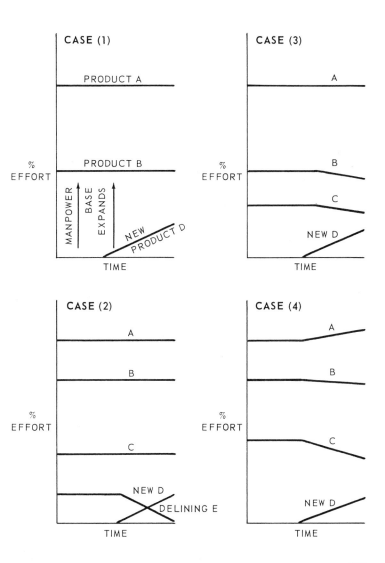

Exhibit 26
Effort Map

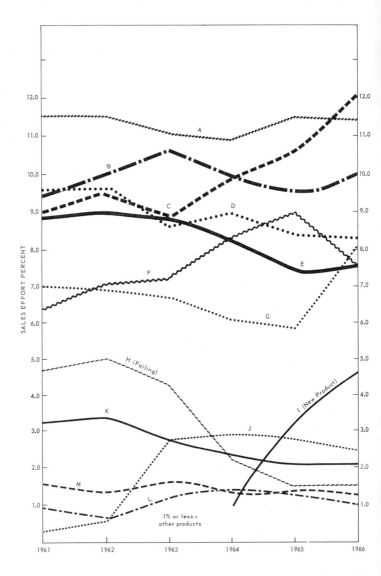

ucts. However, it is difficult to tell which products were actually affected by this factor and which were not. In addition, the analysis developed in Chapter 5 on the factors that motivate sales indicates that there are other factors, such as demand/supply ratio and competitive pricing, that influence sales and, in turn, effort. What role did these factors play? An analysis of the effort applied to all the company's products over time would be less difficult if it had always acted to control effort applied to products, but the cause-effect relationship would still not be clearly drawn. In the Appendix, two methods are described for measuring the effects of effort changes.

The determination of the financial effects of new product introduction may be particularly important under conditions of sales manpower rationing. In this case, the decision to market the new product would hinge on the expected profitability from the new product and the calculated opportunity cost due to effort siphoning. Thus, a set of decision parameters could be developed:

IF: Expected profit on new product > opportunity cost
 THEN: Market the new product
IF: Expected profit on new product < opportunity cost
 THEN: Do not market the new product

The opportunity cost should be included in the evaluation of all ventures when manpower rationing conditions exist.

Game Theory

Game theory is an important field in operations research. It is possible to translate gaming models that have been developed for other marketing variables, such as advertising, into a technique for solving marketing staff-

Exhibit 27
The Prisoner's Dilemma Game

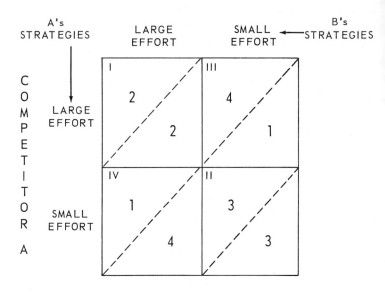

COMPETITOR B

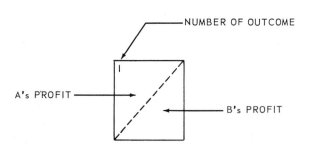

ing problems. In general, gaming techniques are mathematically sophisticated, and it is recommended that only individuals with an extensive mathematical background be employed to develop them. Let us examine some relatively simple gaming models and their potential usefulness in marketing staffing applications.

The Prisoner's Dilemma Game. A game that has been used by the author to illustrate competitor interaction is often referred to as the Prisoner's Dilemma Game. (See Exhibit 27.) In this game there are two competitors, A and B, who attempt to gain profits by using sales effort. To simplify the model, the competitors sell only one product, and all other factors (such as price and advertising) are equal. Each competitor has two marketing strategies:

1. To use a LARGE amount of sales effort.
2. To use a SMALL amount of sales effort.

Since each has the choice of using two strategies, there are four possible outcomes:

I	A LARGE,	B LARGE
II	A SMALL,	B SMALL
III	A LARGE,	B SMALL
IV	A SMALL,	B LARGE

In outcome I, both competitors have incurred a high but equal sales cost. Therefore, their profits are equal but low. In outcome II, both competitors have incurred a low but equal sales cost. Therefore, their profits are still equal, but are higher than in outcome I. Both these outcomes represent situations in which each of the competitors has gained an equal share of the market at equal cost. These outcomes are referred to as "competitive equilibrium" situations. In the case of outcome III, Competitor A has incurred a high sales cost, but because Competitor B used SMALL sales effort, A obtained a larger market share and higher profits (in fact, higher profits than in outcome II). Conversely, in outcome IV, Competitor B obtained a larger market share and higher profits. For easy reference, the four outcomes are usually presented in the matrix form shown in Exhibit 27.

The game begins as each competitor chooses a strategy *without knowing what the other competitor is choosing.* Suppose that Competitor A is very anxious to obtain a large market share and is willing to spend the money to deploy a LARGE sales effort. Competitor B feels that in the long run it would be desirable to obtain an equal market share at a small sales effort level (thus conserving sales effort resources) and decides to deploy a SMALL sales effort. The result would be outcome III, and on a four-point profit scale where 1 is low and 4 is high, A receives a profit of 4, and B receives a profit of 1. In the first round, A has won.

Now the two competitors choose strategies again. A wants to keep up his winning ways and repeats LARGE sales effort. Although B recognizes that outcome II is preferable for both, he is forced to increase his sales effort to LARGE to avoid another bad round (B assumes that A will repeat his bid). The result is outcome I, in which both A and B receive a profit of 2.

Under some conditions it is likely that both competitors will continue to repeat their LARGE bids. In this case, neither competitor is willing to bid SMALL, because of the risk that the other competitor will take a larger market share; each competitor assumes that the other will not immediately follow his lead to bid SMALL. Experienced marketing men would probably make an attempt to reach the higher but equal profit of outcome II. Legal restrictions prohibit competitors from agreeing with each other to bid SMALL in order to reach the mutually advantageous outcome II. However, one competitor can "signal" the other by making the move to the SMALL level and hoping that his competitor will follow in the next round.

The Prisoner's Dilemma Game is very interesting, because it accurately reflects competitive interaction. Of course, other variables like price or advertising expenditure can be substituted for sales effort in this example. Other gaming models that can be adapted to sales effort management include those developed by: Sasieni, Yaspan, and Friedman;[1] Mills;[2] and Shakun.[3]

The Sasieni-Yaspan-Friedman model. The model developed by Sasieni, Yaspan, and Friedman is classed as a zero-sum, two-person game. The expression "zero sum" refers to a game in which whatever one person wins the other loses. The net total, therefore, is always zero. This relatively simple game involves two competitors, A and B, who have fixed amounts available for spending on sales effort. The marketing region is divided into any number of sales districts. In each of the sales districts there is a fixed sales potential. It is assumed that sales performance is proportional to the sales effort applied. The problem is to determine the optimum sales effort strategy for each competitor to maximize sales.

The competitors have an infinite number of courses of action open to them under these conditions, and the deriva-

---

[1] M. Sasieni, A. Yaspan, and L. Friedman, *Operations Research Methods and Problems* (New York: John Wiley Sons, 1966), pp. 176–178.

[2] H. D. Mills, "A Study in Proportional Competition," *Mathematica,* December 1959.

[3] M. F. Shakun, "A Dynamic Model for Competitive Marketing in Coupled Markets," *Management Science* 12, no. 12 (August 1966), pp. B-525-530.

tion of the solution depends on the theory of "continuous games." The best strategy for each competitor is to spend sales effort in proportion to the sales potential; the resulting total sales of each competitor will be proportional to the amount that each spent on sales effort. This problem is simple enough to solve by intuitive means, but the mathematical theory is important in solving more complex games.

The Mills model. Mills developed the "theory of competitive equilibrium," covering the influence of advertising expenditure on brand competition, and including manufacturing costs and the income from sales. Both competitors attempt to apply sales effort to maximize their profit. The expenditures of the two competitors on sales effort should be proportional to the unit profit margins on the products. The competitive equilibrium can then be determined in terms of the two competitors' profits. It is interesting that the competitors' total profits vary as the cube of their unit profit margins in this example.

The Mills model is a static model that obtains noncooperative equilibrium solutions for sales effort expenditures in the case of two or more competitors selling a single product in a fixed or variable total volume market.

The Shakun model. Shakun considered a variable market volume and obtained a two-competitor, fixed-market, single-product result as a special case of the two-product model. He developed a model for a market that is "coupled" in the sense that the sales effort expended by Competitor A on product X influences the sales of product Y (also sold by Competitor A). This coupling effect can be considered in terms of sales effort applied at a specific account. That is, the sales effort applied to sell one product at that account influences the willingness of the account to purchase other products. In this dynamic model, any number of competitors and products can be treated.

Optimization Techniques

Operations research techniques like linear and non-linear programming have been used extensively for solving distribution problems. A common distribution problem of this type is the determination of the optimum location of warehouses and plants, and transportation routings between them. Optimization techniques can also be used for other kinds of routing problems that are related to marketing staffing, particularly the routing of salesmen through their sales territories.

It is well known that the typical salesman, especially the industrial salesman, spends a significant portion of his time in traveling to the accounts in his territory. In many cases, travel time may represent 50 percent of total sales time. The cost of travel can be considered in terms of the direct cost of salary and overhead plus travel expenses, and in terms of the opportunity cost incurred when sales calls are missed because of inferior travel logistics. In most companies, it is left to the salesman to determine his call pattern, and operations research techniques are rarely used to optimize the logistics of his territory.

One approach that can be adapted for this purpose is the Traveling Salesman Problem, a characteristic problem that can be solved by assorted mathematical or heuristic techniques. In its simplest form, the method of solution may involve visual observation; in more complex cases, the use of very large computers is required.

The basic problem concerns a geographical area and

various accounts located in that area. The travel time, distance, and cost between each pair of accounts are known or estimated. The time required at each account is also known or estimated. The salesman is then required to leave an origin point and to call on some or all of the accounts in the territory. The Traveling Salesman Problem solution is resolved by determining the minimum travel time, cost, and distance to cover the chosen accounts and the optimum route or sequence of sales calls on these accounts. Various techniques available for solving the problem include:

1. Mapping and visual observation.
2. Simple computer techniques.
3. Complex computer techniques.

In many cases it is best to use less complex methods, since the additional time and cost of complex techniques may be greater than cost savings from improved logistics. A mapping and visual observation technique is described by Maffei.[4] In this method, base maps for appropriate metropolitan areas were obtained from the United States Department of the Interior, and a clear plastic sheet was affixed to the face of each map. The maps were then gridded into 150×150 foot squares. All customers were located on the maps, and each was assigned a unique ten-digit code that referred to the location. Account information (including location, class of trade, average purchase volume, delivery pattern requirements, dollar sales, and special characteristics) was kept on punched cards.

With the salesman's territories arranged in this man-

[4] R. B. Maffei, "Modern Methods for Local Delivery Route Design," *Journal of Marketing* 29 (July 1965), pp. 13–18.

ner, it is possible to appraise by visual inspection the degree of logistic optimization. In other cases, it may be necessary to use more complex computer techniques. Although many examples of the Traveling Salesman Problem refer to delivery schedules in which the value of each account by location is essentially the same (for example, in milk delivery), it is usually possible to reflect the varying value of customers and potential customers to model a salesman's territory realistically.

5

The Economic Justification
for Sales Effort

THE objective of this chapter is to examine the economic basis for using sales effort. In the field of economics this would be referred to as microeconomic analysis. Most college graduates who have had a course in macro- and microeconomic analysis are more interested in macroeconomics, because it relates to problems of a national economy. On the other hand, microeconomics, with its focus on price theory and the behavior of the firm, is usually considered unrelated to the student and consequently very dull. Unfortunately, many individuals retain this belief that microeconomics is too theoretical and unrelated to their business careers. If the microeconomics course were given to a group of marketing men, it would be of extreme interest, because *microeconomic theory is basic to nearly all real marketing activity.* This preface is necessary, because the very mention of words such as "oligopolist" often produces a violent reaction from those marketing men who retain an impression of their college experience.

The typical industry in the United States can be characterized as a pure or a differentiated oligopoly. The pure oligopoly involves a few sellers that produce identical products and supply the entire output of an industry. Each of the sellers represents a significant fraction of the total industry output. In a differentiated oligopoly, the outputs of the few sellers are differentiated in that the product of each is a close but not perfect substitute for the others. Thus each seller enjoys a degree of monopoly in that his product is different from rival sellers' products.

Since the typical United States firm is usually an oligopolist, it is valuable to consider the role of sales effort in the oligopolist's market behavior. Much of the casework presented in this book deals with the pure oligopolistic marketer. It should be noted, however, that the pure oligopoly is a theoretical extreme and that product differentiation is present in nearly all real market environments.

Sales Effort as a Nonprice Competitive Weapon

In microeconomic analysis or price theory, a standard analytical method is to describe the quantity demanded of a company (sales) in terms of the variables that influence that demand. For example:

$$Q_x = f\ (P_x, P_y, Y, T, W, P_o, S)$$
$$(Company\ A)$$

The statement reads that the quantity of product X

demanded of Company A (sales) is a function of the price of product X (P_x), the price of product Y (P_y), income (Y), taste (T), wealth (W), average price of other commodities (P_o), and sales effort (S). The normal procedure is to hold constant all but one variable in order to evaluate the relationship between demand and one variable, although in the real world all variables operate simultaneously.

It is valuable to consider the relationship of sales to sales effort when all other factors are held constant, and to examine sales both by individual seller and as a total industry demand (see Exhibit 28). At the constant price levels, the demand curve will *shift* as sales effort is added or subtracted. That is, an increase in sales effort by one seller will increase his sales; this increase will be in part due to increased industry demand and in part due to sales taken away from rival sellers. In a real situation, the other sellers may also change sales effort or other variables. Thus the outcome is often difficult to determine (see Chapter 6). It is important to define those conditions under which a change in sales effort by one seller will result in increased profit to that seller, for this is the key to the successful management of sales effort.

Competitor Reaction to Sales Variables

It is important to consider the situation in which a change (in this case, an increase) in sales effort by one seller does *not* cause competitor retaliation. The one seller (Competitor A) increases expenditure for sales effort and expects sales and profits on those sales to increase by an amount greater than the increased sales effort costs. Even if we assume that other competitors "stand pat," the in-

118

Exhibit 28
Industry and Single Firm Demand Curves
For an
Oligopolist Under Changing Sales Effort Conditions

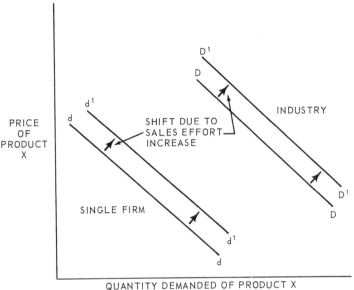

QUANTITY DEMANDED OF PRODUCT X

crease in net profits to Competitor A will depend on the degree to which the product can be differentiated from the same products sold by the competition. If we assume that the competitors sell products of equal quality, at an equal price, and the buyers consider the products to be essentially identical, then the effect of Competitor A's sales effort increase *may* be nominal. On the other hand, if the products are somewhat different or can be made to appear different, then the effect of increased sales effort *may* be significant. The word "may" is emphasized for a specific reason. The economist might argue that when products are equal in all respects, the buyer focuses on price. Furthermore, because the buyers are price-conscious and buy to specification, product differentiation and sales promotion cannot be important. However, as a consequence of the sensitivity of sales to price in markets where products are essentially equal, competitors' prices tend almost inevitably to become identical, and no widely announced price differentials are likely to be sustained. With prices stabilized, then, what determines competitors' market shares? One key factor is sales effort.

Case studies have indicated that in product markets where it is difficult to differentiate a particular seller's product, sales effort is a less effective or less efficient influencing force than other weapons like price, but when these more powerful forces, or power factors, are neutralized by collusive competitor action, sales effort becomes an effective means of influencing sales. It is important to recognize that, under product market conditions where the power factors are active, the addition of sales effort will be fruitless. The wise marketer will act to neutralize these power factors and then apply sales effort to increase sales and market share.

At this point it is reasonable to ask, "Why use sales effort; why not operate with the power factors?" The fact is that the use of price tactics, a relatively powerful marketing weapon, may result in substantial gains *and* substantial losses. Moreover, the experienced marketer will state that it is far easier to become involved in a *declining* price war than an *increasing* one. Reducing price tends to increase sales volume, but unit profits are decreased if fixed costs are less than variable costs. The trade-off in price changes is in terms of sales volume versus unit profits.

Another problem involved in the use of price versus

sales effort is the time lag between weapon action and competitor response. A list price change is known by all competitors immediately. A price change at a particular account is known by competition within days. A change in sales effort, however, may not be detected by a competitor for months or even years. The effect of sales effort increases may not be as powerful under conditions of equal time lag, but may be much more so if the difference in time lag is significant. To be sure, sales effort or advertising will be matched by rivals as surely as will price reductions, but less easily, less quickly, and less exactly, thus giving the individual marketer a better chance to gain an advantage.

Relative Influence of Competitive Weapons

The marketer must be able to predict the future use of competitive weapons in order to determine the amount of sales effort that should be planned. The past activity of competitors in a product market may furnish a guide to the future. Regression analysis, discussed in Chapter 4, provides a guide to the past effectiveness of sales effort and the amount of influence of other factors. But it is the marketer's responsibility to discover what these other factors are. One approach is to use multiple regression analysis to rate the relative influence of competitive weapons. Another, more simple method is to reduce the number of influencing variables to a few key parameters that represent most of the variables and can be readily measured. For example, a list of suspected influencing variables can be drafted (Exhibit 29). This list can then be reduced to three factors: product selling price, demand/supply ratio, and sales effort.

Exhibit 29
Factors That Influence Sales

1. Activity of competition, including salesman effectiveness, pricing policy, technical backup effectiveness, and character of the firm.

2. Effectiveness of the firm's salesmen and supporting sales personnel.

3. Pricing policy of the firm.

4. Effectiveness and amount of technical service backup.

5. Image that the firm has established on the basis of performance.

6. Effectiveness and amount of product promotion.

7. World economic condition.

8. U. S. economic condition.

9. Local market economic condition.

10. Success or failure of the firm's customers to expand the demand for "downstream" products (industrial-intermediate type of products).

11. Distribution capability of the firm.

12. Interproduct competition.

13. Product quality.

14. Product availability.

15. Political influence such as pollution and health legislation.

16. Company relations.

Selling price. The selling price should be related to competitive forces in the marketplace. Interproduct competition and competition from other marketers (both basic producers and resellers) should influence the selling price of one competitor to a significant degree. A decline or decrease in selling price should indicate that competitive pressure is increasing; an increase in selling price should have indicated a relative lessening of competition. It is apparent from Exhibit 29 that actual pricing is only one of the possible competitive weapons that can affect a competitor's selling price; in instances where there is an imperfect match in other competitive forces, the competitor's selling price may be affected through attempts to offset competitor advantages. That is, if a seller is considered by the buyer to be a better source of technical information and assistance, it may be necessary for a rival seller to reduce the selling price to counter this competitive advantage. If competition takes the form of a competitive product, similar changes in selling price may be required to equalize the product's economic advantages to the buyer. In general, the selling price can be considered to be representative of a large number of influencing factors, and can be cited to indicate the condition of the marketplace at any given time.

Demand/supply ratio. The national demand/supply ratio is representative of many influencing variables. We mention the national D/S ratio rather than that of a particular seller, because the latter has an influence mainly on the particular competitor, while the former is characteristic of all competitors.

The D/S ratio is important because it relates to two important market factors. Product *demand* can be considered to be a measure of the local, national, and world economic conditions; of the technical acceptability of the product; of the significance of political influence such as pollution and health legislation; and of the success or failure of the buyer in expanding the demand for the product in second-generation products (in this case, we refer to an industrial product which is an intermediate in the industrial cycle).

Product *supply* can be considered to be a measure of the producer's production capacity constructed to balance the product demand.[1] It is considered "normal" for competitors to maintain excess capacity in order to avoid continuous capital investment, to obtain advantages from economy of scale, and to provide capacity for rapid sales expansion. Since each seller more or less allows for capacity in excess of the real sales increases, the magnitude of the national capacity surplus reflects the current and future marketing activities and policies of the sellers.

Sales effort. It should be reemphasized that sales effort can be regarded as an important factor when other, more powerful factors have been neutralized through competitor interaction. This "neutralized" marketplace is characterized by (1) a demand/supply ratio that approaches an "ideal," where capacity is sufficient to meet the fluctuations in demand but is not excessive to the extent that competitors experience severe economic pressures; and (2) a selling price that is in line with historical product cost-performance criteria and reasonable profitability. In other words, the neutralized market can be thought of as one in which the competitors are relatively satisfied; or if not satisfied, then willingly inactive through disinclination to provoke competitor reaction.

---

[1] "Supply" in this argument refers to plant capacity rather than to the "willingness of sellers to supply" that is normally used in microeconomic theory.

Evaluation of the three variables. The three parameters —selling price, demand/supply ratio, and sales effort— can be matched against sales performance to determine which factor was most influential in a particular time period. A simple trend-matching technique could be utilized over a historical period. A particular case study, conducted by this method, involved six products over a six-year period. A typical product chart is shown in Exhibit 30. In this particular study it was determined that of 24 cases (12 involving constant sales) the D/S ratio was the key variable in 13 cases, sales effort was key in 7, and selling price was key in 4. If we assume that this study is applicable to other industrial products, it is interesting to compare the results with our previous discussions of economic concepts.

It should be noted that selling price was the least important factor. This tends to amplify the conclusion that, in pure oligopoly markets, price is usually the same (even though it is the most powerful weapon when used), and that sales are therefore influenced by nonprice factors. Actually, price competition in oligopoly markets takes place primarily at specific accounts under conditions where the list price of all competitors is the same. We would underestimate the degree of price competition by considering only list prices; it is important to look at actual selling prices.

The fact that the D/S ratio is the most important variable should not be surprising, since sales performance and demand go hand in hand. Since supply shifts generally occur in a stepwise fashion with most competitors increasing capacity simultaneously, the number of cases (years) in which the ratio would decrease sharply (and not be matched by a decline in sales) are relatively few. The significance of the D/S ratio is that the forecasting of

Exhibit 30
Three-Parameter, Trend-Matching Analysis

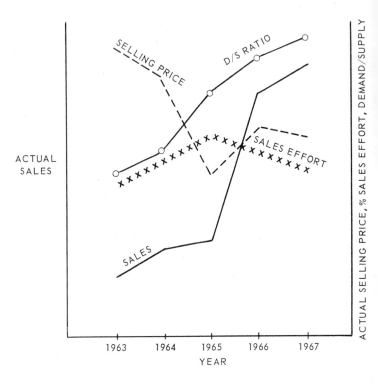

national demand is critical in predicting the sales performance of an individual seller. Although market share may be improved through wise marketing tactics, a good portion of each seller's sales growth will depend on the seller's ability to capture newly created demand.

Having determined the historical pattern of influencing variables, we return to the key issue. It is important, in planning the future use of sales effort, to evaluate how efficient and how profitable the use of that sales effort will be.

126

Marginal Cost = Marginal Revenue = Maximum Profits

It is desirable to continue to add sales effort (that is, increase costs) until the point at which the marginal cost equals the marginal profit; at this point, the firm's profits will be maximized. This simple statement should be regarded as a theoretical premise. In actual practice, it is nearly impossible to determine this maximum profit point, because the environment is exceedingly complex. Yet the statement points in the right direction.

Marginal cost is the easiest element to determine. In most instances, the calculation of the marginal costs associated with recruiting, hiring, training, and deploying a new salesman will serve the purpose. Consider the simple case of a firm selling one product with one salesman. The sales manager must decide whether the firm's profits will increase if he adds another salesman. He does not have to decide the number of salesmen required to maximize profits; he calculates the marginal cost of adding a new man and needs only to forecast marginal revenue. Using a regression analysis of past effort and sales, which indicates that sales have responded efficiently to sales effort, he performs a historical analysis of other factors that have influenced sales and finds that sales effort was most important. He decides that the market will grow because of the technological benefits of the product, and although he does not know whether national demand will be increased by increased sales effort or whether his two competitors will change their levels of sales effort, he feels that if the competitors match his sales effort increase, the consequent amount of increase in national demand split three ways will not give sufficient marginal revenue to equal marginal costs.

The sales manager must also take into account the possibility that his sales effort increases might be countered by a competitor's price reduction. He might well construct a "decision tree" to assist in evaluating the possible outcomes of his staffing decisions. Yet he cannot even determine the marginal revenue under the conditions where the competitors "do nothing." Being a modern thinking management scientist, he depends on the historical regression data and modifies it slightly to reflect future market conditions. He estimates "probability of occurrences" for each of the events on the "tree," estimates the "payoff," determines the "expected values," and decides to add the salesman. After one year, sales have increased and the sales manager feels confident that he made a wise decision.

But one must still ask, "Did marginal revenues exceed marginal costs?" Or more simply, "What was the amount of increased profits due to the addition of the salesman?" The company economist points out that the national economy performed at a higher rate than expected. One of the salesmen reports that a competitor had some problems with its warehouse deliveries. Another says that one of the competitor's experienced salesmen retired and an inexperienced man replaced him. The finance manager reports that high manufacturing costs caused the unit profit on the product to decline. The laboratory manager reports that one competitor fired half of the technical representatives who assisted the salesmen. The sales manager is told by the company's largest customer that it has given more business to the company than it deserved, in order to make up for the previous year when the buyer felt that he had short-changed the company. It would not be surprising if the sales manager's confidence in his decision declined to the point at which he was not sure what had really taken place.

This simple case can be made much more complex, and yet it points out the difficulty in using the three-part equation, MR = MC = profit maximization. The marketing environment is complex; the future is highly uncertain; and yet decisions on sales effort must be made.

Static and Dynamic Demand Models

Most of the capable works that have been published in the field of microeconomic theory include only a brief discussion of the effects of sales promotion on the demand schedule for a firm. In addition, "sales promotion" is often treated as advertising in consumer markets. We are concerned with developing a model with regard to sales effort (particularly in industrial markets) and we want to explore the use of sales effort in pure oligopolies when prices are equal.

Classical price theory deals primarily with a static demand model; the consideration of dynamic demand models is a relatively recent development coinciding with the progress in game theory. The need to consider dynamic models rather than static models is clear when we attempt to investigate oligopolistic competition, since the reactions of competitors affect the performance and hence the strategies of the firm.

The classical static demand model for oligopolistic competition is the "kinked demand curve" (Exhibit 31). The discontinuity of the marginal revenue curve and the kink in the demand curve reflect the influence of competitor reaction. If the firm raises its price above p, it is assumed

Exhibit 31
Oligopolist's Kinked Demand Curve
Under Conditions of Competitor Reaction

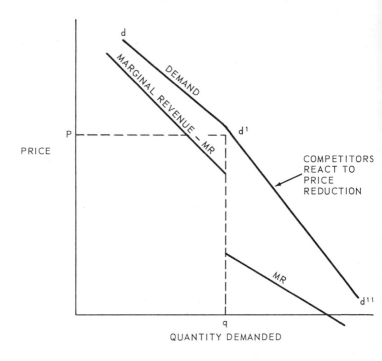

that rival firms will not change price and the firm's sales will follow the line $d'd$. When the firm decreases price below p, it is assumed that the rival firms will match (or beat) the reduction and that sales will increase by a lesser amount per unit price change along the line $d'd''$. The marginal revenue received by the firm, therefore, is positive and high above p, and low or negative below p. In the case where the firm's marginal cost is less than the marginal revenue when the price is greater than p, and

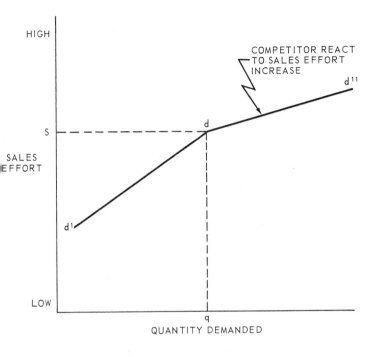

$MC = MR$ when price is less than p, the firm will maximize profits at p—provided that at this price the relationship of price to average cost allows what is regarded as "fair" or satisfactory profit.

The kinked demand curve can be applied to a sales effort/demand curve in an analogous manner (Exhibit 32). We should expect the slope of the demand curve to be more gradual, since sales effort is a less powerful weapon than price. The reasoning follows that if a firm decreases sales effort from the equilibrium point s, the other competitors will not change effort and the sales of the firm will drop off rapidly along d'd. When the firm increases sales effort, it is assumed that other competitors will match the increase, thus forcing the firm to follow the demand curve dd''.

The static model thus developed is fixed, not only in time, but also with regard to the changing behavior of the firms, which may be related to their organizational goals. In Chapter 6 a dynamic model is presented that reflects the real marketplace.

This discussion of the economic justification for using sales effort is probably the most difficult section of this book to absorb, partly because the thoughts communicated are highly concentrated and involve an unusual jargon for the typical marketing man. It may be well to reread this chapter after a period of time, in order to reinforce the reader's grasp of its real significance. The author believes that microeconomic analysis is the essence of marketing and sales effort management; if it is clearly understood, it can be an invaluable aid to the alert marketing manager.

6

The Dynamic Marketing
Strategy Game

In CHAPTERS 3, 4, and 5, the subject of sales effort management was examined in terms of behavioral, quantitative, and microeconomic analysis. In one sense, these chapters provided the basic groundwork for attacking the "real" world of marketing, which is the daily environment of the marketing manager. It is a highly complex environment in which simple "cure-alls" never work. The marketing manager has suffered through contacts with numerous individuals who have no marketing experience but think that they understand the function, and appear disappointed with the seemingly irrational way in which the marketing manager deals with marketing problems. They may talk a great deal about how they can improve upon the poor, muddled marketing manager's performance, but when they are given a chance to enter the marketing field, these critics either fail miserably or gain a new awareness of the difficulties involved in marketing.

Marketing is a complex field, because there are so many variables that affect decisions and the results of those decisions. Any mathematical model that reflects the total system is, therefore, complex. Total marketing models are not written in several pages; they are written in books. Some of the world's most gifted mathematicians and systems analysts have thrown up their hands at the prospect of dealing with the marketing system. But despite all the frustrated attempts, talented individuals are always developing new techniques that offer an opportunity to get closer to the heart of the problem.

One approach is to start with a descriptive, qualitative model of marketing activity and to design this model in a way that can lead toward a quantitative representation. Such a qualitative model will be developed in this chapter. The objective is to describe accurately the real interaction of competitors that is at the center of marketing activity. The first priority is to describe the real marketplace and not a simplified version of it. If a quantitative method cannot immediately be developed to translate this real qualitative model, we will at least have made progress toward a meaningful analysis of marketing behavior, using the qualitative model as a valuable educational tool. As more attention is devoted to developing real quantified models, the approach may evolve into a deterministic tool.

In developing a marketing strategy game, the marketing analyst should follow a series of steps aimed at an in-depth understanding of the product and product market. Let us assume that a company has decided to test the value of a marketing strategy game. Although the company has a multiproduct line, the test will be conducted on one

134

product. A hypothetical case study can be formulated in which the selection of a product to model is the first step in the model building process.

Selection of the Product

When the study team gathered opinions from various managers, it discovered a controversy over the selection of a product to model from a product line of 50 products. In many instances, the manager's recommendation appeared to be based on special interest in the product, rather than on an in-depth analysis of the value of the product to the proposed model. But the study team was finally able to make a selection, and the product and product market that they chose could be characterized as follows:

1. There were three competitors.
2. The three competitors sold approximately equal amounts.
3. The economics of the three competitors were relatively equal.
4. Product quality was essentially equal.
5. Historically, the market shares of the three competitors had been essentially constant, and each competitor's sales had grown at the rate of 5 percent per year over the last ten years, because of growth in the economy.
6. The three competitors were established in the market and were regarded as sophisticated marketers.
7. The three competitors were large corporations and for practical purposes had infinite resources to contribute to the product, provided that cor-

porate investment criteria were exceeded.

8. There were a large number of customers, and the concentration of buyers was low.

9. There was no dominant end-use for the product; the use of the product was broadly based.

10. The market had high barriers to entry, because in order to achieve competitive economies of scale, it was necessary to manufacture and market several derivative products.

11. The national demand for the product was highly correlated with the Federal Reserve Board (FRB) index (correlation coefficient approximately .98).

The selected product was analyzed in terms of the study team's objective: to build a model that would lead to improved understanding of future sales volume and average return for the company. First, it was apparent on the surface that this product and its market were relatively tidy. The three competitors seemed to be at equilibrium, and sales increases were due to industrial growth. The surface description did not reveal the active competitive struggle that was also characteristic of this product. Therefore, the market could be considered a very active, competitive one that was continually achieving equilibrium. As to the relative advantages of this product, the following comments were offered:

1. The relatively small number of competitors greatly simplified the possible competitor interactions and resulting outcomes. Another product, which was rejected for the model, had 15 competitors.

2. The fact that the competitors had equal market shares, equal costs, and equal quality products indicated that no major differences existed between competitors

that would make the game one-sided. For example, if there were significant cost advantage, the game would tend to be price-oriented, since the competitor of lowest cost would lead price down to gain market share. However, the significance of the "equal share" equilibrium versus the "one competitor with largest share" equilibrium was not important.

3. The fact that the competitors were established and could be considered sophisticated led to the assumption that competitor behavior would be partly based on historical data and could be regarded as intelligent and rational. (It is very difficult to deal with irrational behavior or on behavior that has no basis in the past. This is part of the new-entry dilemma.)

4. The fact that there were a large number of customers and that they were not concentrated was very important to the company's ability to predict future sales and average return. In the past, attempts to model the largest customer in hopes of reducing the uncertainty of the most significant variable had not been fruitful.

5. The fact that many end-uses existed was important for the sensitivity of sales to environment changes in one large end-use. Attempts at modeling the end-use had not been successful.

6. The existence of relatively high barriers to entry reduced the probability that a new entry would occur over the planning horizon.

7. The existence of equal economics had to be considered as historical data. Future reductions had to be allowed for as well, but the nature and scale of the industry mitigated the possibility of radical cost reductions in the future. On the other hand, the industry had a highly technological basis that could lead to some cost reduction.

8. The fact that the market share was stable over time,

and that the market itself was growing at 5 percent per year allowed for competitor demand increases by capturing new growth or winning business from other competitors.

9. The high correlation with the FRB index provided a strong support for forecasting future national demand. Also, the national demand was not as sensitive to marketing expenditures as it would be in the case of a consumer product. That is, if advertising, technical service, and sales effort were cut off, there would still be a high level of demand. (In industrial marketing, the buyer was considered to be rational about establishing a product need on an economic basis; consequently, it would not cancel orders if all the salesmen did not call.)

10. The equal quality removed the problem of quantifying "quality," which had been difficult in the past.

11. The fact that the corporations were large removed considerations of resource rationing; therefore, the decision on resource addition was based on return-on-investment criteria only.

There were also product characteristics that tended to make the model more difficult to construct. Primarily, the problem centered around the sensitivity of manufacturing costs of the studied product (A) to new processes for manufacturing a product B. Of the total amount of product A produced, over half was used to manufacture product B. It was not economical to make only product A, so the economics of producing A depended on the market for B as well. A new process manufactured product C and produced, as a byproduct, product B. The market dictated that the new plants be built with an emphasis on product C; product B would be sold at a low price, replacing sales of product B derived from product A. Therefore, it was necessary to predict the inroads of product B produced in the new plants and, more elementary, to predict the market growth for product C.

The selection of a product to model should be based on this kind of rigorous analysis. The value of microeconomic analysis is apparent in this case. As a general rule, it is best to select a product that has relatively simple market characteristics, that is, "simple" with regard to the variables that would influence the mathematical complexity of the model if it were quantified. Of particular importance are the number of competitors and the influence of factors not controllable by the competitors.

Weapons of Competition

When experienced marketing personnel were questioned with regard to the weapons that competitors used, the following list was developed:

1. Price.
2. Sales effort.
3. Technical service.
4. Distribution facilities.
5. Advertising.

Price. The prices charged by competition included:

- List prices.
- Distributor prices.
- Competitive prices.
- End-use prices.

List prices were on a delivered basis and varied with the quantity per shipment and the type of container. In

Exhibit 33
Alternative Price Actions

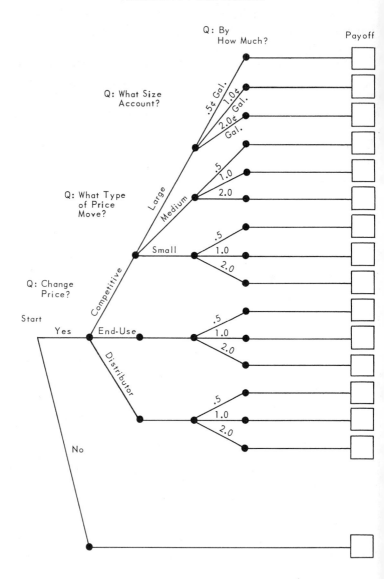

general, the price charged for large quantities was x, the price for medium quantities was x plus 3 cents per gallon, and the price for extra-large parcels was about x minus 5 cents per gallon, but varied with the shipping destination. Small quantities shipped in special containers were sold at x plus 18–40 cents per gallon. Since most of the shipments were in price category x, this price was used as a base price for the model. In order to give the distributors an incentive to market products, they were given a discount of about x minus 5.5 cents per gallon.

As a result of the Robinson-Patman Act, competitors were limited to (1) meeting a bona fide competitive price at an account, or (2) establishing an end-use price that would apply to all buyers at a given end-use.

In order to construct a model that realistically portrayed market price activity, a set of possible competitor price moves was developed (Exhibit 33). A payoff was generated for each competitor for each move, and then the payoff was modified according to competitor responses in that round (this will be detailed later). Also, a current set of prices was furnished at the start of the game.

Sales effort. Sales effort in this study was composed of (1) the gross amount of time spent by a salesman in a direct discussion with the buyer concerning product *A*, and (2) the effectiveness of the salesman in the time period. A relatively sophisticated system existed for recording each salesman's actual time by product on a quarterly basis. The time spent in traveling, in the office, or in other nondirect selling activities was omitted. The effort on product *A* was reported as a percentage of total sales district effort.

The degree of effectiveness was always difficult to measure in a quantitative manner, particularly in an industrial marketing context. However, it was decided to hypothesize the average salesman and to assign an increase in sales effort and an expenditure of money for salesman training, over and above pre-field-assignment training. The alternative competitor actions with regard to sales effort are presented in Exhibit 34.

Technical service. Technical service involved the expenditure of monies by the seller to assist the buyer in solving technical problems within the buyer's operation. This device was used primarily in industrial products marketing, and represented a considerable part of total marketing expense. For example, an industrial marketer might spend five times as much on technical service as on advertising. The return on investment for technical service had not been studied to any extent, and the complexity of the problem had made it difficult for companies to evaluate technical service effectiveness. Surveys of historical expenditures on technical service led to the set of alternatives in Exhibit 35.

Distribution facilities. Throughout the history of the industry there had been a continual improvement in distribution capability, primarily in response to the competition of direct sellers and distributors. It had been demonstrated that a competitor who was always able to deliver on a "next day" basis would outperform a competitor who could deliver on that basis only half the time. This was the case even when the customer had ample product storage capacity to afford a week's lead time on reorders. The alternative competitor actions with regard to distribution facilities are outlined in Exhibit 36.

Advertising. The relative importance of advertising in an industrial marketing context was radically different from that in consumer marketing. It was typical for an industrial marketer to spend about 0.2 percent of sales revenue on advertising. There were several reasons for

Exhibit 34
Alternative Sales Effort Actions

A. GROSS TIME

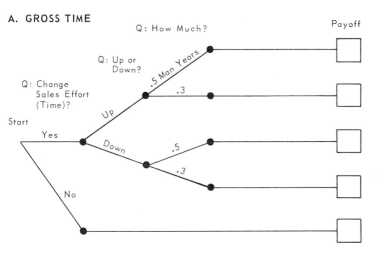

B. EFFECTIVENESS

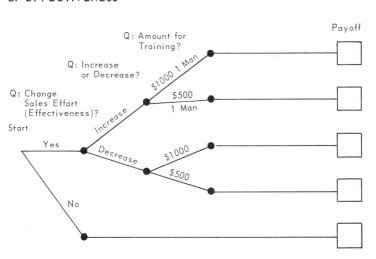

143

Exhibit 35
Alternative Technical Service Actions

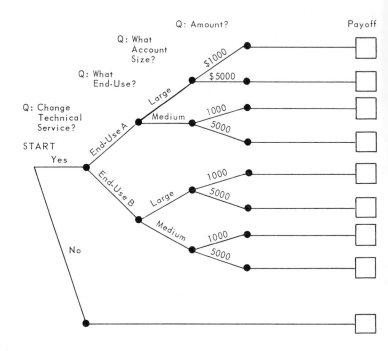

this. First, the number of buyers was comparatively small and, therefore, mass media techniques were inefficient. Second, the buyer's decision to purchase was relatively rational, and he was less likely to be influenced through advertising. Third, the era of the expensive gift to buyers had passed, and many purchasing agents were reluctant to accept free pens. Fourth, the effect of industrial advertising on sales was nearly impossible to estimate. The office cabinets of industrial sales managers were packed with Starch readership plaques; they remained unconvinced that this proved anything. The industrial marketer spent

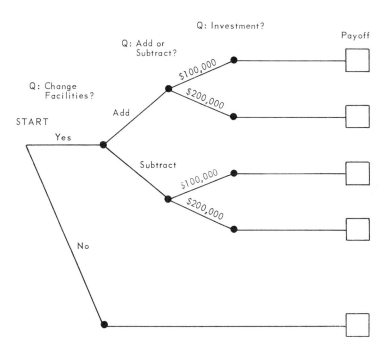

Exhibit 36
Alternative Distribution Facilities Actions

Q: Investment?

Q: Add or Subtract?

Q: Change Facilities?

Payoff

START

Yes

$100,000

$200,000

Add

Subtract

$100,000

$200,000

No

a token amount on advertising to keep in the industrial view, in hopes that the odd buyer, who was passed over by the field salesman, would respond to the ad. The alternative competitor actions are outlined in Exhibit 37.

The Game Plan in Brief

In order to present the analysis of competitive interaction in a meaningful manner, it is necessary to outline the overall game plan as it was conceived. Basically, the

Exhibit 37
Alternative Advertising Actions

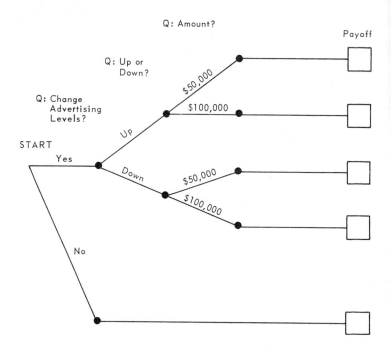

game would involve three competitors, each having one bid or opportunity to alter a competitive weapon in each round. The round would end when each competitor had been polled once. The competitors would be provided with historical data on their past sales, on their competitors' past sales, on market shares, on end-use mix by competitor, on price levels, on manufacturing costs (theirs only), on sales effort (theirs only), on technical service expense (theirs only), on distribution facilities, on advertising expense (theirs only), and on national industrial statistics. Unfurnished data referring to competition would

146

be obtainable, but the accuracy of the information would be in doubt. The competitors would study the actual data and other information on each company so that they could understand the particular company's attitude.

Time lag would be built in so that the effect of a competitor's action would be in accordance with observed market response. The competitors would have the option to change some parameters in every round (for example, price), but would be restricted by a repeat time limit for changing other parameters (for example, distribution facilities). Again, the idea was to reflect the real market. Capital investment in production facilities was also permitted. Each player's performance was summarized periodically.

It should be noted that the study team was mainly concerned with the development of a realistic model that could be used by persons interested in observing the complex marketing environment. No attempt was made to develop an elaborate game structure complete with behavioral science analysis.

The Effect on Demand, Average Return, and Profit

The essence of developing a realistic model was the analysis and construction of output response to input variations. For example, how was the effect of the following round determined?

Competitor 1—decreased price, competitive, large account, 1.0 cent per gallon.

2—increased price, distributor, 0.5 cent per gallon.

3—passed.

It could be reasoned that in terms of demand:

- Competitor 1 would gain business at the large account, since no one matched, and would pick up distributor business because of 2's price increase.
- Competitor 2 would lose business at the large account and lose distributor business.
- Competitor 3 would lose large account and gain at distributor.

In terms of average return:

- Competitor 1—average return down if:

$$\frac{Dol_1 \cdot Rol_1}{Dot_1} \frac{Dx_1 \cdot Rx_1}{Dot_1} > \frac{Dnl_1 \cdot Rnl_1}{Dnt_1} \frac{Dx_1 \cdot Rx_1}{Dnt_1}$$

Where Dol_1 = old demand at large account (Competitor 1)
Dot_1 = old total demand (C_1)
Rol_1 = old avg. ret. at large account (C_1)
Dx_1 = remainder demand (C_1)
Rx_1 = remainder avg. ret. (C_1)
Dnl_1 = new demand at large account (C_1)
Dnt_1 = new total demand (C_1)

- Competitor 2—average return down if:

$$\frac{Dol_2 \cdot Rol_2}{Dot_2} + \frac{Dod_2 \cdot Rod_2}{Dot_2} + \frac{Dx_2 \cdot Rx_2}{Dot_2} >$$

$$\frac{Dnl_2 \cdot Rnl_2}{Dnt_2} + \frac{Dnd_2 \cdot Rnd_2}{Dnt_2} + \frac{Dx_2Rx_2}{Dnt_2}$$

Where Dod_2 = old demand at distributor (Competitor 2)
Rod_2 = old avg. ret. at distributor (C_2)
Dnd_2 = new demand at distributor (C_2)
Rnd_2 = new avg. ret. at distributor (C_2)

- Competitor 3—avg. ret. down if:
  [Same as Competitor 2.]

This reasoning, however, did not answer the key questions regarding the quantitative effects. The study team approached this problem by developing a series of demand curves for each competitor, reflecting the influences of competitor response within weapon type, such as price versus price and sales effort versus sales effort. A sample curve is shown in Exhibit 38. Rigorous questioning of the sales department staff supplied a set of reasonable price-volume relationships that accurately reflected the real marketplace.

In the case of sales effort, the intuitive approach developed for price was supplemented by the use of historical data on changes in sales effort and sales volume in the sales districts. Straight-line regression equations were derived to measure the correlation between changes in sales effort and changes in sales.

Although there was no disputing the fact that saturation effects would set in at some point, the key was to determine the point at which the marginal profit on additional sales equaled the marginal cost of the extra salesman, and it was hypothesized that this point was at some distance from saturation. Also, the difference between linear and nonlinear models within realistic sales effort ranges was felt to be too insignificant to justify the added complexity of nonlinear models. In any event, the historical relationship of sales effort and sales for a given product might be matched with an intuitive impression of a favorable response to salesman's efforts, indicating that, for all its complexity, the use of sales effort tactics could reap rewards.

The team recognized that the effect of competitor in-

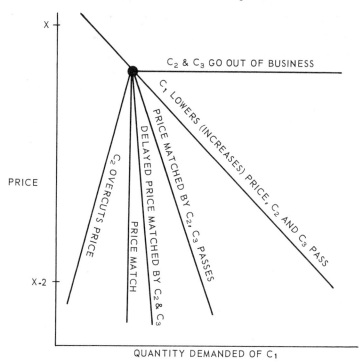

Exhibit 38
Competitor C_1 Demand Schedule
Under Various States of Competitor Response
In a Given Round of Bidding on Price

teraction within weapon type on profits could be determined by subtracting relevant costs from gross revenues. This could be done on either an annual or a longer term basis, with the inclusion of the concept of the time value of money. Thus the investment in a salesman might include training expense plus salary in year one without any return, while in future years the profit on sales attributable to the salesman might be considerably in excess of costs. A discount rate could be chosen as a decision criterion in determining the size of the sales force.

Interweapon Effects

In the real market environment, competitors met in interweapon as well as intraweapon conflict. The complexity of deriving demand versus variable curves under different competitor interactions was compounded when the possibility of interweapon conflict was included in the model. It was necessary to rely largely on intuitive judgment by experienced marketing personnel, since it was not possible to obtain historical data on isolated interweapon competition. Complications included unequal time lags of competitive weapon type. For example, if Competitor 1 chose to increase technical support while Competitor 2 chose to increase its sales force, a true measure of interweapon competition (technical support versus sales effort) could not easily be determined, because the influence of technical support expenditures on sales might take effect one quarter in advance of the sales force increase effect. To cloud the issue further, still another variable might be introduced within the time lag. A general demand curve was derived, however, to approximate the real market (see Exhibit 39).

One conclusion was that the best approach was to study the historical correlations of a weapon with sales, in order to predict future behavior on the basis of estimated future changes in the market environment. It was recognized that the use of correlation might average the effects of inter- and intraweapon competition, as well as other

Exhibit 39
Competitor C_1 Demand Schedule
Under Interweapon Competitive Actions

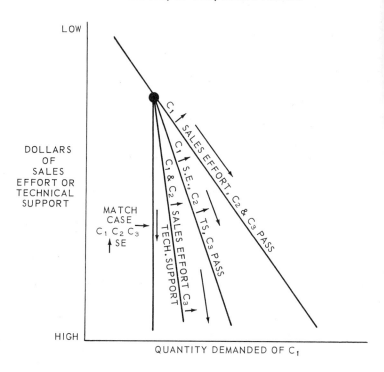

influences such as demand/supply conditions, but it was decided that until more comprehensive quantitative approaches were developed, this might well be the best method of approaching the problem.

The New Entry

Most marketing men understandably regard the prospect of a new entry with suspicion. Marketing is an exceedingly complex environment, and it is likely that the new entry will add considerably to this complexity.

The new entry is basically an unknown. More specifically, the goals of the new entry are not known, nor is the cost structure, sales force capability, technical support competence, or pricing strategy. It is often possible, however, to predict the new entrant's future behavior. The pessimistic marketer assumes that the new entry will cut price in an attempt to secure a market position and utilize plant capacity. The current marketers will either have to compete on a price basis (thus sacrificing their past success in developing a sales force and effective technical support activities) or move over and let the new entry secure a part of the market. In sharp contrast to textbook descriptions of the demand-expanding effects of the new entry, allowing all competitors to prosper, the experienced marketer knows that the demand is rarely elastic enough, given the minimum economic plant size of the new entry. This is particularly true in mature product markets.

Is it possible to model realistically the three competitor interactions of the new market, given that the fourth competitor may have an unusually disruptive effect on the individual demands of the three historical competitors? Although this question is quite controversial, the new entry can probably be modeled within the limits of the original game model. Even though the new entry chooses a different weapon mix and changes price in large increments, the effect on demand can be obtained through a consideration of expanded demand schedules, including wider variable limits. Again, although the new entry may reduce price below costs to gain a foothold, the demand curve for any of the old competitors should not be discontinuous; it should be only an extension of the demand curve applying to C_2 and C_3 competitive responses. However, this is not to say that the demand curve will not be a different shape in the extended regions, or that the derivation of these extended curves will be a simple matter.

Future Plans

The study team concluded that the game description reflected the real marketplace, but that the quantitative determination of scheduled demand was subject to considerable uncertainty. Therefore, it was suggested that the game's primary use be education, in that both marketing and nonmarketing personnel could increase their understanding of the marketing process by using the game model. It was concluded that the game would result in a better understanding of the factors that influence the determination of probability distributions in both future sales volume and average return, and would lead to improved venture analysis and product management.

7

The Final System Design: Sassafras Phase 2

Up to now, we have considered a particular case study, attempted to develop a conceptual framework for marketing staffing decisions, and derived numerous analytical techniques to improve the quality of the staffing decision. The preliminary system design (SASSAFRAS Phase 1) was developed to function in the current organizational environment. Because the system worked around these environmental constraints, the performance of the system was expected to be suboptimal. We did not anticipate that the output of SASSAFRAS Phase 1 would lead to the selection of the optimum number of salesmen in optimum locations.

If we consider a future time period and desire to improve on the crude staff projections of Phase 1, it is possible and reasonable to design a better system, a system that will lead toward better staffing decisions. Because the design is for the future, the constraints of the Phase 1 environment are not present, and it is possible to change the internal organizational environment, although the external environment will be much more difficult to influence. In other words, we begin SASSAFRAS Phase 2 design with the recognition that the organization, policies, procedures, plans, and attitudes can be changed to provide an internal environment in which SASSAFRAS-2 can perform. Suffice it to say that if the members of the organization are not willing and able to change the environment, the decisions concerning marketing staffing will be inferior.

Defining the System Mission

In connection with SASSAFRAS-1, it was stated: "The basic system mission is to determine optimum field sales force levels for the next four years." The primary criterion to be used in this determination was: "... profitability. ... To continue to add salesmen if the present value profit of that investment discounted at the cost of capital is positive." This basic mission is also appropriate for SASSAFRAS Phase 2.

At this point it is worthwhile to consider a rival criterion mentioned during the implementation of SASSAFRAS-1: "Determine the potential profitability in each territory and add salesmen until the profitability is zero." In essence, the difference between the two criteria is that one focuses attention on a minimum acceptable profit situation while the other attempts to generate a rank order of total territory profit. In terms of our ability to predict the future, the minimum-oriented criterion is much more reliable. However, under manpower rationing conditions, it is desirable to have a rank order of potential territory profitability. The minimum-acceptable criterion does not value one territory over another, as long as the criterion is met.

In Phase 1 design, two system subgoals were defined:

1. To optimize the salesman's performance in a logistic sense.
2. To provide guidance to the field sales organization concerning product profitability.

Again, these subgoals are meaningful to Phase 2.

The basic mission and the two system subgoals were achieved to a limited degree in Phase 1; in Phase 2, the basic mission will be approached in a stepwise fashion, since each year's system output will be more accurate as the system itself and the internal operating environment improve.

The salesman logistics subgoal was not achieved to any extent in Phase 1. It was possible only to pick out those sales territories that were extremely disjointed and that forced the salesman to operate inefficiently. Detailed analysis of salesman logistics was difficult to obtain from a head office location. The local manager was in a key position to perform this analysis, but unfortunately, the local manager did not have enough time or knowledge to determine logistic efficiency and to improve the territorial logistics. In Phase 2, this subgoal will receive increased attention to improve sales performance.

The product profitability subgoal was achieved to a limited extent in Phase 1. An inherent problem with product profitability information that is generated at the head office for head office use is that it is not tailored to the local district. In most cases, the profit information is too general. The local manager must receive profit data that are relative to his district in terms of actual overhead costs, actual sales discounts, distribution costs, entertainment expenses, salaries, and so on. The achievement of this subgoal will be stressed in Phase 2.

Before we discuss subgoals that were a part of Phase 1 and are still relevant, or that are new goals, it is essential that we point out the need for and value of obtaining relevant information. It should be noted that the first step in system design is to determine what information is required, where it can be found, how it can be obtained, and also how much it costs. The failure of Phase 1 (suboptimal performance) can be attributed to bad or deficient information and human failure. There is a great temptation for practitioners to spend more effort on developing unique ways of using data than on the what, where, how, and how-much questions about the information. A competent job of data gathering will go a long way toward problem solution; therefore, much of the design for Phase 2 will focus on approaches to developing a relevant data base for manpower decisions. In a nutshell, Phase 1 admitted that the information was poor but that the system mechanisms performed anyway; Phase 2 will be concerned with using many of the same system mechanisms but with better data. The differences between Phases 1 and 2 are mostly in the area of data quality.

One system subgoal of Phase 2 is to build effective, self-adapting mechanisms into the operating description. In essence, the self-adapting process depends on selecting data in the environment that are critical to system performance, in developing methods to determine how the system should be changed, and in setting operating rules to change the system in the desired manner. It is hoped that the critical environmental information will act as leading indicators rather than unmeaning data.

It is desirable to have sufficient time to change the system to maintain system capability. For example, if we were concerned with sampling the environment in a baseball game to alter pitching system performance, it would be disappointing if our data collection consisted in counting the number of home runs given up to opposing teams. Clearly, by the time we recognized that the rate of home runs was increasing and recommended that the pitching system be changed, the system performance would be adversely affected because of the time lag (although the number of runs might still be decreased after the system change).

It has been demonstrated that it is valuable for SASSA-FRAS, not only to recommend a total number of salesmen, but also to advise head office sales management on the location of salesman additions. It is also desirable to recommend salesman product mix or effort division by product and to evaluate the benefit of concentrated end-use selling.

The three stages of system design (analysis of the current system, system constraints, and system requirements) have been covered in Chapter 2 in the preliminary system design. The current marketing staffing system has been critiqued. The system constraints for Phase 2 are considered minimal, since the system is designed for a future time and no constraints have been set for the future. The system requirements are unchanged from Phase 1, although these requirements were only partially achieved in Phase 1.

Defining the Future Operating Environment

Some general conclusions can be drawn with regard to the future operating environment of SASSAFRAS-2. Previously, we discussed the problem of monitoring the environment to gain understanding of future possibilities. It is necessary to predict the operating environment from a given point in time, even though we recognize that the prediction is sensitive to changes in the environment.

An industrial marketer today, predicting the environment in the next four years, might conclude the following with regard to marketing staffing:

1. The number of manufacturer-marketer competitors will increase.
2. The number of manufacturer-marketer competitive salesmen will increase.
3. The number of distributors and distributor salesmen that compete against the manufacturer-marketers will increase.
4. The competitors' salesmen will be better trained.
5. The salaries of salesmen will be higher.
6. The distribution costs in terms of rail, truck, and ship will increase if increased labor costs of terminal and warehouse operators, truck drivers, and so on are not matched by more efficient methods and more automated operation.
7. The amount of competition from foreign companies will increase.
8. The competition will be more sophisticated, particularly with regard to decisions based on quantification of data.

9. The growth in the economy will not be as rapid as in the last five years.
10. The cost of products will increase or decrease depending on the labor-automation trade-off.

In essence, the future industrial marketing environment is going to be rougher in nearly every way. This is a continuation of a trend that began to gain momentum in the early 1960s. In this short period, several of the "glamour," high-return industries have been under tremendous pressure. The rate of change of technology has sharply reduced the period of high profits in the product life cycle. The companies that have prospered have literally been designed around the expectation that things will change very rapidly. The manager concerned with marketing is under increasing pressure to counter some of the technological factors that have tended to turn new products into obsolete products. The marketing group receives from development groups fewer and fewer products that are easy to market because they "sell themselves" on performance alone. Most often the marketer must succeed with a product that is "equal to competition." With increasing frequency, marketing is asked to "save a project" by selling an inferior product. To the marketing manager faced with this current and future environment, the subject of staffing is of vital concern.

Developing a Relevant Data Base

In developing our data base, we must be concerned with determining what data are required, where the data are located, how the data can best be obtained, and how much the data will cost.

I. SALES EFFORT DATA

What. The first order of business is to develop good information on how the salesman spends his time. It is essential to have an accurate accounting of time spent by each salesman at each account by product. Further breakdowns that would be helpful but are less essential include time spent by end-use and time spent by class of account. A refinement of time spent might consider the *intensity* of the time spent, although this invites bias in the reporting.

Where. The information is available from the individual salesman. Attempts to have inside district personnel or, worse, head office personnel estimate time spent should be discouraged.

How. It is unfortunate that the salesman, who is the only reliable source of the effort data, is a very busy individual. In addition, salesmen have continuously resisted and complained about the increasing use of their time for paperwork. Aside from this personal dislike, time taken for paperwork reduces the time spent in actual sales calls. Therefore, the method of data gathering must involve as little of the salesman's time as possible, and be as little objectionable as possible. Of the various methods considered, the best is to have the salesman put the information on an IBM card. The data reporting format on the card would be kept very simple and involve a minimum amount of writing. The card could be used to record market intelligence information as well. Thus an existing marketing information reporting system involving dictated call reports and summaries of customer buying patterns could be eliminated and replaced by the single data card.

Keeping the data on cards offers many advantages in recording, collating, and presenting the data at the district and head office level. One possible format would use mark-sense cards which would require the salesman to pencil in data. The advantage of mark-sense cards is that they can be optically scanned rather than keypunched. Although the salesman would be expected to resist this "further inroad of paperwork," he should be able to fill out a card in thirty seconds to one minute, if customer codes and the like are readily available.

How much. The cost of setting up an effort reporting system, processing the cards at monthly intervals, and printing would be minimal. The cost of salesman's time would also be small if the time per card were one minute or less.

II. SALES TERRITORY DATA

What. It is important to obtain information on the following for each sales territory:

1. Product sales potential mix.
2. Account size mix.
3. Geographic location of accounts.
4. Travel time between accounts.
5. Number, capability, age, and experience of competitive salesmen.
6. Number and location of competitor sales offices, distribution facilities, and manufacturing facilities.
7. Buying attitude (measured as probability of success in selling) of important accounts.
8. Strategies of competition (such as price and sales effort) in the local market.
9. Profitability on sales by product and account.

10. Profit potential by product and account.
11. End-use mix.

Where. All items except 9 and 10 are obtainable from the sales districts. Additional information from the head office must be supplied to determine 9 and 10.

How. In general, the information can be obtained by the salesman. The district manager's assistance would be valuable in items 7 and 8. If a district has an inside salesman or sales analyst, he can gather and compile much of the data, thus saving the salesman's time for direct selling. Items 1–6 and 9–11 need to be covered annually. Items 7 and 8 should be appraised continually, although written documentation is required only when a major change is evidenced.

How much. The cost to obtain sales territory data is primarily dependent on the cost of human resources required to generate the data. The effort expended will be concentrated prior to the submission of the annual appraisal and will be insignificant during the rest of the year.

III. PRODUCT PROFITABILITY DATA

What. It is desirable to obtain product profitability information that is pertinent to the particular sales district and the sales territories in the district. It is valuable to have profit information based on the selling price to an account in the district, the distribution costs to the customer, the amount of technical support furnished to the account, and the district overhead, travel cost, entertainment, and other sales costs relative to the account. These costs, excepting distribution cost, are in part or totally under the control of the district. Manufacturing costs, on the other hand, are not. The two costs must be included to measure absolute profitability, but should be accounted separately in order to measure district performance. It is valuable to determine profits on both actual sales and total potential sales.

Where. Costs other than those related to manufacturing are obtainable at the district level. Distribution costs can be obtained locally or from a head office traffic department. Manufacturing costs are available at the head office.

How. The cost data should be obtained from the district manager rather than from the salesman, since many of the costs apply to the overall district operation. Costs should be reported initially and when appreciable changes occur. It is worthwhile to have the district manager forecast costs and then to measure actual costs regularly with the forecast costs. It would be useful to put cost data relating to specific accounts on cards to simplify data handling. Manufacturing costs could be obtained from head office reports.

Utilizing Data in the "Profit" Subsystem

In Chapter 2, the subsystem PROFIT was designed to "provide guidance to the field sales organization relative to product profitability." The data base designated "product profitability" should be used to accomplish this purpose. The purpose of the PROFIT subsystem is not to supply the raw profit data. The system designer or equivalent must translate the raw data into parameters that reflect local circumstances. It is important to account for district and territorial differences in terms of distribution costs, selling costs, and sales discounts.

The use of profitability data for manpower planning purposes brings up questions about the use of the data. It may not be desirable for other reasons to use profit data for sales decisions. Therefore, the local manager will be forced to use data for one purpose and to "forget" it for others. It is questionable whether product profit guidelines to the district should be in exact cents-per-pound figures that would include short-term irregularities in manufacturing costs. It may be best to use a base manufacturing cost that has been smoothed. If the manufacturing cost is relatively constant, the smoothed data will be a reasonable approximation of the real data and permit the analysis of other costs.

In SASSAFRAS-1, the PROFIT subsystem output consisted of high, medium, and low profit categories. This type of guidance may be acceptable if the incremental differences between products can be categorized in such a manner. If profits vary widely or are skewed, the high-medium-low breakdown will be misleading.

The operating rules for the PROFIT subsystem can be written as follows:

1. System Designer:
   Obtain from data bank (Exhibit 40) product profitability information, including
     - Weighted average selling price in sales territory by product.
     - Weighted average distribution cost in sales territory by account (also by product if difference is significant).
     - Technical support expenditures in sales territory by product and by account.
     - Sales district overhead.
     - Sales travel time (costs), entertainment expense, salary, and so forth.
     - Smoothed manufacturing cost data.
2. System Designer:

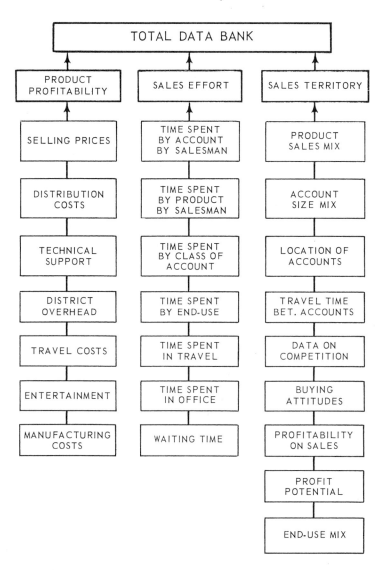

Exhibit 40
Data Bank Subsystem

TOTAL DATA BANK

PRODUCT PROFITABILITY

- SELLING PRICES
- DISTRIBUTION COSTS
- TECHNICAL SUPPORT
- DISTRICT OVERHEAD
- TRAVEL COSTS
- ENTERTAINMENT
- MANUFACTURING COSTS

SALES EFFORT

- TIME SPENT BY ACCOUNT BY SALESMAN
- TIME SPENT BY PRODUCT BY SALESMAN
- TIME SPENT BY CLASS OF ACCOUNT
- TIME SPENT BY END-USE
- TIME SPENT IN TRAVEL
- TIME SPENT IN OFFICE
- WAITING TIME

SALES TERRITORY

- PRODUCT SALES MIX
- ACCOUNT SIZE MIX
- LOCATION OF ACCOUNTS
- TRAVEL TIME BET. ACCOUNTS
- DATA ON COMPETITION
- BUYING ATTITUDES
- PROFITABILITY ON SALES
- PROFIT POTENTIAL
- END-USE MIX

167

Calculate the product profitability for each sales territory.

Let: Product profitability of product $X =$ PP_x

Weighted average selling price $= SP_{xwa}$

Weighted average distribution cost $= DC_{xwa}$

Technical support $= TX_x$

District overhead $= DO_x$

Salesman expenses $= SE_x$

Smoothed manufacturing costs $= MC_{xs}$

Then: $PP_x = SP_{xwa} - (DC_{xwa} - TS_x - DO_x - SE_x - MC_{xs})$

3. System Designer:

Calculate the total profitability of each sales territory.

Let: Total actual profitability of sales territory $= P_{ta}$

Sales volume of product $X = S_x$

Then: $P_{ta} = \Sigma\, PP_x S_x$

4. System Designer:

Calculate the total potential profitability of each sales territory and the profit market share. It is essential to know the actual and potential profitability so that market share can be determined.

Let: Actual sales volume $= S_s$

Potential sales volume $= S_p$

Then: $\Sigma\, PP_x S_p =$ Total profit potential $= P_t$

Assuming: $PP_x = PP^1_x$

Where: PP^1_x is the profitability of product X in the unsold portion of the market.

The profit market share is then determined by

$$P_{ms} = \frac{P_{ta}}{P_t}$$

168

5. System Designer:
   Present data to sales manager for approval to distribute information.
6. System Designer:
   Transmit data to district manager.

Utilizing Data in the "Salesman" Subsystem

In Chapter 2, the subsystem SALESMAN was designed to "optimize the salesman's performance in a logistic sense." This subgoal could be thought of as a process of improving salesman logistics to make them more optimal. We are concerned here with how the salesman utilizes his time in carrying out the sales activity in his territory. In general the analysis must be performed at the district level, although methodology supplied by the head office may be helpful. The type of logistic problem that can be solved by application of the methodology used for the Traveling Salesman Problem (see Chapter 4) is rarely pertinent to the industrial marketer. In cases where the value of each account is similar, call frequency is equal, and a call pattern can be devised, the approach used in the Traveling Salesman Problem may be valid. However, the operating rules of the SALESMAN subsystem will deal both with Traveling Salesman Problem situations and with those cases where the application of the method is not particularly useful.

Basically we are concerned with the assessment of salesman's time spent in calling versus his time spent traveling, working in the office, entertaining, and preparing for calls. It is important to determine the best allocation of the salesman's time in the various activities. We are also concerned with how the salesman uses the available call time. We recognize that the time spent in speaking to purchasing representatives depends in particular on the geographic location of the accounts, and is inversely related to travel time or distance between accounts. Although each territory is unique, there are general approaches to improving the efficiency of salesmen within given territories, as well as to rearranging territories to achieve more efficient district solicitation.

IN SASSAFRAS-1, the output of SALESMAN depended on the district manager's appraisal of logistic efficiency. In most cases, there was not enough time to analyze territories thoroughly and, consequently, the most obvious inefficiencies were the only ones treated.

The operating rules for the SALESMAN subsystem can be written as follows:

1. System Designer:
   Obtain from data bank sales territory data, including
   - Account size mix and location of accounts.
   - Travel time between accounts.
   - Account buying attitudes.
   - End-use mix.
2. System Designer:
   Obtain from data bank sales effort data, including
   - Time spent by account by salesman.
   - Time spent by class of account by salesman.
   - Time spent by end-use by salesman.
   - Time spent in travel by salesman.
   - Time spent in office by salesman.
3. System Designer:

Prepare traveling salesman map (see Chapter 4).

- *Obtain* base maps from the U.S. Department of the Interior (or other suitable source) of geographic areas matching sales territories.
- *Grid* the maps and *Locate* accounts on the grids.
- *Classify* accounts by code to include class, end-use, current sales by product, potential sales, current and potential profits, buying attitude, competitor activity, and call frequency.
- *Measure* distance between accounts and *Estimate* travel time.

4. System Designer and District Manager:
   Visually Inspect the traveling salesman map; *Access* the degree of logistic optimization within territories and among all territories in district.

5. System Designer, Sales Manager, and District Manager:
   If logistics can be improved, *Rearrange* territories or sales solicitation pattern within territories.

6. System Designer, Sales Manager, and District Manager:
   If logistics cannot be improved, *Do Nothing*.

7. System Designer:
   Compile profiles of time allocation by salesman, including:
   - Time spent in direct confrontation with purchasing representatives.
   - Time spent in waiting in customer's reception area.

- Time spent in traveling to and from accounts.
- Time spent in district office.
- Call time spent by end-use.
- Call time spent by class of account.

8. System Designer and District Manager:
   Compare profile with logistic map of sales territory. *Recommend* changes in time allocation to improve logistics and to maintain reasonable ratio of office and out-of-office time.

9. System Designer:
   Compare salesman profiles and *Determine* reasonable time allocation guidelines.

10. System Designer and Sales Manager:
    Transmit orders to change time allocation profiles by salesman.

Forecasting the Future

In the operation of SASSAFRAS, it is necessary to make forecasts of the future. The major forecast areas and their primary use are as follows:

1. District Manager:
   Forecast sales potential growth and market share for use in determining economic value of salesman investment.

2. System Designer:
   Forecast the sales manpower requirements for new products to be introduced over the next five years for use in scheduling manpower deployment.

3. System Designer and Recruiting Director:

Forecast "leakage" in recruiting, hiring, training process (see Chapter 2) for use in setting recruiting goals.

4. System Designer and Sales Manager:
   Forecast "leakage" in field sales force due to transfers, dismissals, retirements, resignations, and military leaves for use in setting recruiting goals and planning for incoming transfers from other sources.

5. System Designer and Sales Manager:
   Forecast competitor activity in areas of sales force deployment and utilization of other competitive weapons for use in determining the size of the sales force.

6. System Designer and Sales Manager:
   Forecast the general economic conditions, legislative regulations, changes in end-use technology, and any other conditions that influence product demand, for use in determining the response to sales effort.

7. System Designer, Sales Manager, District Manager, Manufacturing Manager, and Distribution Manager:
   Forecast sales volume, selling prices, and costs for projecting product profitability.

NOTE: The various forecasts can be contained in a separate FORECAST subsystem (see Exhibit 41).

Developing Sales/Effort Response Ratings

The economic value of applied sales effort can be thought of in terms of product profitability and response

Exhibit 41
Forecast Subsystem

FORECAST

SALES POTENTIAL GROWTH
AND MARKET SHARE

SALES MANPOWER FOR
NEW PRODUCTS

RECRUITING, HIRING, TRAINING
PROCESS "LEAKAGE"

FIELD SALES FORCE
"LEAKAGE"

COMPETITOR ACTIVITY –
USE OF COMPETITIVE WEAPONS

ECONOMIC CONDITIONS,
LEGISLATIVE REGULATIONS, ETC.

SALES VOLUME, SELLING
PRICES, COSTS

to sales effort. That is, case studies using regression analysis (see Chapter 4) have shown that the change in sales volume for a given change in sales effort for a product varies, depending on the mix of competitive weapons and general demand/supply conditions. Therefore, a product may be inherently profitable, but if the sales response to sales effort is poor, low sales volume and hence low profits will result. Product profitability data were developed in the subsystem PROFIT. We now wish to generate sales/sales effort data. The designation of this subsystem is SALES EFFORT.

The operating rules governing SALES EFFORT are as follows:

1. System Designer:

   Obtain information from data bank to include:
   - Historical time spent on direct solicitation by product by district.
   - Sales performance by district (data smoothed to exclude unusually large accounts).

2. System Designer:

   Apply regression analysis (straight line) to data and *Obtain* regression line and regression parameters. If straight line correlation is poor, use curve-fitting techniques to improve correlation.

3. System Designer:

   Analyze regression data and *Explain* correlation in terms of observations on the use of competitive weapons. Trend-matching analysis may be helpful in this study.

Evaluating the Performance of the System

The integrated performance of the subsystems PROFIT, FORECAST, SALESMAN, SALES/EFFORT, and DATA BANK constitutes the general system SASSAFRAS. Each of the subsystems must function in relation to other subsystems if SASSAFRAS is to exhibit high system performance (see Exhibit 42). The system designer must monitor the information flows between the subsystems. In essence, the system contains a series of operating rules and a specified pattern of subsystem interactions.

Human factors in Sassafras performance. The precise definition of operating rules includes a human designer to carry out the rule. Human failure may limit system performance by affecting the execution of the action orders. A second source of difficulty concerns the human response to the activation of the rules. The performance of SASSAFRAS depends on the acceptance and effective implementation of the system recommendations by management. The ultimate success of the system depends on the individual salesman's ability to perform at average effectiveness. The territory chosen may be highly favorable to profitable exploitation, but if the salesman is a weak operative, the manpower investment may not be profitable.

It has been noted previously that SASSAFRAS depends on a high content of human resources. Therefore, it is essential that human activity be monitored continuously so that potential failures can be recognized early and corrected. Human performance is the key to system performance and must receive the primary attention of the system designer and others who are concerned with the results of system implementation.

Measuring results: a feedback mechanism. Because of

Exhibit 42
Integration of Subsystems

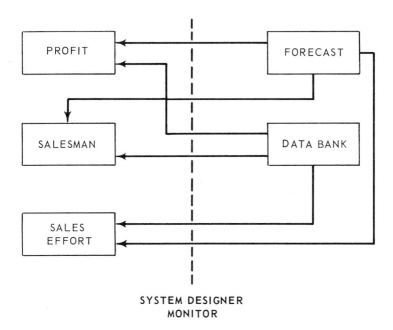

SYSTEM DESIGNER
MONITOR

the nature of SASSAFRAS, it will not be possible to measure system performance for at least one year after execution. It is imperative, therefore, to set up formal feedback mechanisms to report on the profitability of manpower investments that are the results of SASSAFRAS performance. It is necessary to review the manpower decisions annually and to make changes in the SASSAFRAS operating rules where it seems fruitful to do so. It has been repeatedly stressed that SASSAFRAS is designed to change over time; the system designed today may be completely changed at the end of a year's trial period. The fact that the system requires redesign should not be taken as a criticism of the early design but only as a reflection of the changing environment to which SASSAFRAS has been designed to adapt.

Integrating Sassafras into other marketing activities. SASSAFRAS is used for determining the total number of salesmen, but in this operation the system uses information concerning product profitability and product sales/sales effort response. It could be regarded as inefficient not to utilize such data for product planning as well; it is a logical transition to integrate the operation with other marketing activities where the integration would be beneficial. The product managing or planning departments may find sales effort information helpful in deciding marketing strategy. The marketing manager who is concerned with improving total profits over the entire product line may find it helpful to consider both the product profitability and the sales/sales effort response. The new product manager may find the analyses of customers helpful in predicting the success of new product introduction at particular accounts.

The adoption of SASSAFRAS may well lead to more extensive use of the data generated for other purposes. In each instance, management must determine whether the use of the data in other areas can be beneficial, and if so, must design operating systems to accomplish the desired objectives.

Managing sales effort. The author has put forth the proposition that it is a worthwhile objective to manage sales effort rather than to have effort manage the company. In other words, the management of sales effort is considered to be a purposive activity rather than a result of competitor moves or factors outside the company's environment. The dynamic character of industrial marketing competitor interaction has also been described. The conclusion that can be drawn is that a successful marketer must manage sales effort and must manage that effort continuously. It is important to recognize that the effort mix determined today may not be effectual in six months. Sales staffing decisions must never be rigid, but must always be adaptable to the changing environment.

Summary

The major focus of this book has been on the role of sales effort in marketing activity. Although the SASSAFRAS system is designed to improve the performance of the field sales force, the system includes operational functions that relate sales effort to other competitive weapons and to sales performance. Specific chapters of the book attempt to expand the concept of sales effort by considering its behavioral, quantitative, and microeconomic aspects. One chapter is designed to demonstrate the dynamic character of marketing activity by use of a gaming simulation. These chapters provide a disciplined background for designing a system to determine sales force levels.

The system design is carried forward in two phases. The first phase applies to an existing marketing organization, and uses only available information and knowledge. The second phase requires changes in data gathering and work procedures. In addition, the second phase requires that the human resources in the system have a greater comprehension of sales effort and an increased knowledge of modern techniques.

The applicability of the case study. The case study chosen to describe the applicability may not be identical with other situations; obviously, the experience of each marketing organization is unique, and the knowledge level of managers and staff within each organization varies considerably. In order to apply effectively the techniques developed in this study, it may be necessary to change the system design. The case study presented should be regarded as a guidepost and should not be accepted blindly. It is most important to develop a questioning attitude and to discuss the similarities and differences between this case and the case under investigation.

The complexity of the sales staffing decision. To those managers who have made staffing decisions in the past with relative ease, this book may seem to add complexity to a simple decision. It is difficult for them to admit that their decisions were "easy" because much information was being ignored. There is no question that the marketing staffing decision is very complex, and there is no disputing the fact that good decisions can lead to substantial financial rewards to a company, while poor ones can lead to financial disaster. The decision maker must confront and deal with the complexity of his decisions.

The manager who has doubts about adopting a staffing system as "involved" as SASSAFRAS should recognize that his competition may not feel the same way. The manager who does not appreciate the risk he accepts by ignoring his competitors is a gambler who will rarely win.

Marketing: A Discipline in Transition

The history of marketing is dominated by stories of practical men who were successful and of sophisticated theorists who failed. In general, the marketing profession has been the most reluctant to accept modern techniques.

The reasons for this are essentially contradictory. The successful marketing man who was poorly educated and had a restricted knowledge of sophisticated methods would point to the importance of knowing the market and understanding people. The modern marketing man speaks of developing relevant data bases and of considering behavioral science studies. The two types agree on the importance of markets and people, but they cannot communicate effectively because of a significant language barrier.

As more marketing people recognize the language barrier, the sources of conflict between the traditional and modern marketer are resolved. The traditional marketing men, who are now in the power seat, are gradually turning to the modern men for new approaches to the perennial problems. The progress of acceptance is slow for several reasons, but the most important one is that marketing is the most complex of all business functions. The operations researcher does not have the capability, at this point, to solve marketing problems as easily as he might solve transportation problems or capital budgeting decisions.

In a situation where the modern approaches do not always offer superior alternatives to "seat of the pants" decisions, the modern man can easily be rejected by the traditional man in power. The wise marketing man in power will recognize that there is very little hope that "seat of the pants" decisions will improve in the future, while modern techniques are being developed at a rapid rate and are helping to make better decisions even though the improvement in some cases is marginal. The marketing discipline is therefore in a transitional phase. The traditional and modern schools of marketing are involved in an important struggle, and the outcome is clear, although the time scale is still debatable.

The Future

There has rarely been a period of history in which the future was so uncertain. It could be reasoned that only the uncertainty is certain. The acceleration of technology, of social movement, of political development, and of economic disparity has ensured that tomorrow will surely not be like today. Change is the "name of the game." The concept of an accelerating as opposed to a constant-velocity changing environment must be fully appreciated. The marketer who is not "tuned in" to the environment will become a buggy-whip salesman before his time. And yet, the potential rewards to the "tuned in" marketer are greater than in a constant-velocity environment. To most, this challenge is frightening and uncomfortable. The recognition that clinging to the past limits chances for success in the future may be frustrating, but the good marketer must confront the frustration and develop new attitudes. Modern techniques that are keyed to the environment offer avenues to the future.

Appendix

Measuring the Effects
of Sales Effort Changes

(See Chapter 4)

Iɴ ᴍᴇᴀsᴜʀɪɴɢ the effects of changes in sales effort, we believe that it is appropriate to consider both a theoretical method and one that attempts to measure the actual changes in effort.

The Theoretical Method

This method is called "theoretical" because we calculate the effect of effort siphoned off by the new product by assuming that the effect by product was proportional to the effort applied to that product. Thus the real *changes* in effort are not taken into account. The basic steps of the theoretical method are as follows:

1. *Divide* the total effort applied to the new product in a given year by the total effort applied to the studied products; *multiply* this ratio by the effort applied to a particular old product. This gives the weighted effort effect of the new-product effort on the old-product effort.

2. *Divide* the weighted effort effect by the effort on the old product to *obtain* the percent change in effort on the old product. The percent change is constant for all products in a given year.

3. *Relate* the percent change in effort of the old product (caused by the new product) to the old product's percent change in sales by *considering* the regression line (obtained from historical data of percent change in effort versus percent change in direct district sales).

4. *Multiply* the percent change in sales of the old product by the sales volume of the year preceding that in which effort is applied, to *determine* sales volume change. The preceding year is used as a basis because we are concerned with the percent change in sales from that year.

5. *Multiply* the change in sales volume by the annual allocated income unit value for the year. The current year profit is used because the profit effect depends on current profits.

6. *Sum* the profit changes of the individual products to *obtain* the total profit change.

The Actual Method

The complexity of the effort map has been cited with regard to the difficulty in analyzing cause–effect relationships. The actual method attempts to deal with this complexity. The basic steps of actual method are as follows:

1. *Divide* the actual effort on the old product by the total effort on all old products studied, to *obtain* revised effort percentages. This step is necessary if less than the total number of products is considered.

2. *Divide* the absolute incremental effort percent change on the old product by the total absolute incremental changes in effort of all products. Absolute values are used to avoid plus-minus cancelling.

3. *Divide* the results of step 1 by results of step 2 to *obtain*

a ratio that relates weighted effort to weighted incremental effort.

4. *Multiply* results of step 3 by the actual incremental change in effort on the old product to *obtain* a weighted measure. If the actual change is equal in percentage to the effort applied, then the ratio is one and the actual incremental change on the old product remains unchanged.

5. *Divide* the effort on a new product by the total weighted effort changes from step 4.

6. *Divide* the weighted incremental change in the old product (from step 4) by the total weighted increments; *multiply* this by the results of step 5 to *obtain* the amount of new product effort that was subtacted from a given old product.

7. *Divide* the results of step 6 by the amount of effort expended on the old product, to *obtain* the weighted percent effect of the subtraction of effort (because of the new product) from the old product. Unlike the theoretical method, the actual method will show a different percent change in effort for each old product.

8. *Follow steps 3 through 6* of the theoretical method to *obtain* total profit change.

This actual method is one of several that can be derived to evaluate the real effects of effort siphoning.

About the Author

RICHARD V. BUTT is currently the president of Man-Machine Systems, Inc., marketing consultants. Mr. Butt received an engineering degree from Princeton University and an M.B.A. from New York University. Previously, he was associated with Shell Chemical Company, where he was involved with all phases of line and staff marketing activity.